Po ye ge

DOG DANCER

NATIVE AMERICAN DANCE STEPS

by
Bessie Evans and May G. Evans

Frontispiece and Cover Illustrations
by
POYEGE
of San Ildefonso Pueblo,
New Mexico

DOVER PUBLICATIONS, INC.
Mineola, New York

Copyright

Copyright © 2003 by Dover Publications, Inc.
All rights reserved.

Bibliographical Note

Native American Dance Steps, first published by Dover Publications, Inc., in 2003, is a lightly abridged republication of *American Indian Dance Steps / by Bessie Evans and May G. Evans of the Peabody Conservatory of Music / Introduction by Frederick Webb Hodge / Illustrated in Color by Poyege, San Ildefonso Indian*, originally published in 1931 by A. S. Barnes and Company, Incorporated, New York.

The color illustrations originally interleaved with the text have been incorporated into the present cover design; one illustration, reproduced here in black-and-white, now appears as the frontispiece of the book. Typographical changes in the illustrations list, part-title pages, and running heads have been made to conform to these revisions and to the title change.

Library of Congress Cataloging-in-Publication Data

Evans, Bessie, 1885–
    Native American dance steps / by Bessie Evans and May G. Evans ; frontispiece and cover illustrations by Poyege.
    p. cm.
    Originally published: New York, A.S. Barnes, 1931.
    Includes index.
    ISBN 0-486-42700-5 (pbk.)
    1. Indian dance—North America. 2. Pueblo dance. I. Evans, May Garrettson. II. Title.

E98.D2 E9 2003
793.3'1'089974—dc21

2002072874

Manufactured in the United States of America
Dover Publications, Inc., 31 East 2nd Street, Mineola, N.Y. 11501

To

POYEGE and his wife **TAN-TA**
of San Ildefonso Pueblo, New Mexico

———————————————➤✷←———————————————

In appreciation of their friendship
and their coöperation

CONTENTS

CONTENTS

ILLUSTRATIONS

OUTLINE FIGURES OF THE DANCE,

drawn by J. Maxwell Miller under the supervision of the authors:

---※---

INTRODUCTION

INTRODUCTION

>⊛<

I WELCOME the opportunity to express a word of apology for certain pre-conceived ideas that impressed themselves on my mind when, two or three years ago, the announcement was made that the authors of this book were to present an interpretation of the dance steps of some of the Southwestern Indians before the American Ethnological Society. I do not know whether it was due to my own ignorance or to the modesty of the authors in not making their studies more widely known that I gained the impression that what they had to offer would probably be little more than the overdone and misleading impersonation of "Indian" dance movements one so often sees.

I was therefore not alone among those overjoyed by the depth of the study made by the authors, the highly commendable way in which the dance steps were reproduced by Miss Bessie Evans and the verbal interpretations were presented by her sister, Miss May G. Evans. I recall how greatly I had wished that some of my dancing Zuñi Indian friends could have been present and that I could have heard their enthusiastic and generous *Hish hínina!* "Verily the same!", which echoes a deeper sense of appreciation than the words would seem to picture.

Study of the music of our Indian tribes in a thoroughly scientific way has long been in progress, and many have been the adaptations of Indian songs to suit the demands of the white man's ear, often of appealing beauty even if the Indians from whom the themes were derived might fail to recognize them. But in the prosecution of these studies, which include those of the music of Indian dances, a phase of the native culture seems to have been completely neglected until our authors undertook the task of recording and of analyzing it with the graphic and highly successful results of which we are now privileged to obtain a glimpse.

As the reader will observe, the dance steps herein presented offer only a mere hint of the possibilities which the subject affords, for there are still many tribes which have preserved, with characteristic conservatism, at least some of their dances of old. The scientific results which further investigation is bound to yield can well be imagined, for the relation between the actual step and the dance as a component part of a dramaturgic performance, the interrelations of rhythm, the very language which Indian dance steps seem to utter, all promise such a rich store of knowledge that no one can predict at this juncture how far-reaching the study may prove to be.

Therefore let it be hoped that the field which has now been so successfully entered may be further explored and that the importance of the research may inspire the means for extending the investigation.

F. W. HODGE.

Museum of the American Indian
New York City

Native American Dance Steps

FOREWORD

THE FOLLOWING STUDY of American Indian dance is concerned chiefly with elements of the art observed in certain Pueblo tribes of New Mexico—especially those of San Ildefonso, Tesuque, Santa Clara, Cochiti, and Santo Domingo. When, therefore, some phases of the dance are described as "characteristics of the Indian," it should be borne in mind by the reader that they are characteristics observed at least in the Pueblos mentioned. Since it is highly probable, however, that many of the characteristics noted are typical of Indian dance-art in general, it is hoped that the present brief treatment of the subject, representing work in its initial stage, will prove suggestive to students wishing to make more extended research in the future.

The greater part of the material was first presented by the authors, on their return East from the Indian regions, in the form of lecture-recitals at the AMERICAN MUSEUM OF NATURAL HISTORY, the PEABODY CONSERVATORY OF MUSIC, and YALE UNIVERSITY. Acknowledgment of valued favors through which the work was facilitated is made to these institutions; also to the MUSEUM OF THE AMERICAN INDIAN (Heye Foundation) and the MUSEUM OF NEW MEXICO; and, in particular, to the following persons: PROFESSOR GEORGE PIERCE BAKER, MR. JOHN PEABODY HARRINGTON, DR. GEORGE HERZOG, DR. EDGAR L. HEWETT, MR. FREDERICK W. HODGE, MR. J. MAXWELL MILLER, DR. NELS C. NELSON, MR. T. HARMON PARKHURST, MISS HELEN H. ROBERTS, MRS. GEORGE H. VAN STONE,

FOREWORD

and DR. CLARK WISSLER. Especially is it desired to acknowledge the courtesy of many talented Indians, whose product is described herein.

Transcription and analysis of steps and dances are by Bessie Evans; description and commentary are by May G. Evans.

THE AUTHORS

Let them praise his name in the dance.

PSALM 149

Part One

————————————→ ✤ ←————————————

PROLOGUE

PART ONE

>-⊛-<

"A MERE JUMPING up and down to the monotonous beat of a crudely fashioned drum."

In some such manner as this is the casual observer prone to dismiss the subject of American Indian dance-art; regarding it as a quite simple affair and devoid of special appeal or significance. As a matter of fact, it is far more than this. Even the briefest study of the technique and the style of Indian dancing discloses that its steps are varied and often difficult of execution, and that its mood and manner are highly expressive of a peculiar, native genius. It discloses also that the rhythms are diverse, complicated, and marked by frequent change. And, more than all this, it discloses that Indian dance-art is *basically different* from other forms. It is this basic difference, this distinctive expression of racial character, that makes the study of Indian dance and its accompanying song at once baffling and fascinating.

It has always been difficult for the white man to bridge the distance between himself and the North American Indian. This is due partly of course to the naturally great depth of the chasm between primitive man and civilized man; and partly also to the seeming impossibility of breaking down or penetrating the reserve of the Indian. His personality, indeed, is as baffling as his dance-art. So true an expression, however, of his inner self does this art appear to be, so keen is the flash of revelation it brings, that in it the soul of the Indian seems to be laid bare in a greater measure than in any other phase of his personal activity. In his dance and song he is caught, as it were, off his guard.

It is, then, important—even urgent—that this significant American folk-art be preserved and safeguarded. Safeguarded especially from the standardizing hand of the white man; from the tragic deterioration that has been wrought in many other phases of Indian life and product. Happily, the Indian's dance and song have thus far proved to a great extent immune from the blight of the commonplace. Signs are not lacking, however, that they, too, are threatened.

There is, therefore, no time to lose. Dances of all the tribes should be accurately recorded as soon as possible, for fear that in the not distant future they may become altogether extinct; or at least may share a fate similar to that of most of the Indian music now heard on the concert stage—native melody so diluted by the admixture of vocal, instrumental, and harmonic elements supplied by the white musician, as to be virtually denatured. Such use of folk-music has, of course, its rightful and important place in the art of the cultured composer or performer. Its effects are, indeed, often beautiful and inspiring in the case of the free employment of Indian thematic material —however much it may tend to obscure the traditions of authentic native music.

The purely musical element of the Indian's composite art of dance and song has fared better at the hands of scholars than has the element of body movement. Hundreds, thousands, of native tunes of tribes in many parts of the country have been recorded by musicians specially fitted for the task. The melodies have been transcribed by them in as accurate a form as present musical notation permits. Supplementing the work, phonograph records have been made at first hand, by means of which not only the melodic content but the tone-quality and the style have been reproduced with absolute fidelity.

Thus a great body of pure, authentic Indian song has been preserved in permanent form. The world's debt of gratitude to these single-hearted musicians becomes the greater in view of the seemingly inevitable passing of the aboriginal American.

It is to be hoped that laborers in the field of Indian research will ultimately be moved to do as much in the case of Indian dance-art. Hitherto, efforts in this direction have been confined chiefly to the ritualistic, the symbolic, the musical, and the dramatic elements of Indian ceremonial; in which phases profound and detailed research has been made by eminent scholars.

It must be admitted that it is not easy to convey adequately by word, tune, diagram, or picture, the indefinable but distinctive mood of a dance. These aids can, nevertheless, do much to enable the student to assemble the various parts into a form that has a fair degree of fidelity to the original. Something more vivid, more dynamic, however, is needed in order to inform the substance with the spirit. There are qualities in the ceremonial dances of the Red Man that must be personally seen and heard and felt; for of them is born the elusive charm that defies analysis or description. This is true of the dance-art of any race; but especially of one so removed in thought and culture as a primitive people like the American aborigines.

Supplementing personal observation and abstract study, mechanical means are now available—or at least are rapidly being developed—that are capable of providing a very fair substitute for actual first-hand performance. Such little as has already been accomplished in this direction by moving-picture drama is at least highly suggestive of the possibilities. And this, notwithstanding the fleeting and fragmentary glimpses thus far afforded by films that are usually so speeded up that the dancers in them seem bent chiefly on scurrying out of the picture with indecent haste. With a proper application, however, of modern inventions for the synchronization of movement, sound, line, and color, it should soon be possible to reproduce Indian dances in complete and permanent form. With the aid also of "slow-motion photography" the technique of the art could be analyzed and thus made available to students everywhere.

It may be objected—on good ground—that there is a very real obstacle in the way of accurate and complete recording of the ceremonials. That obstacle is the Indian's own distrust—also on good ground!—of the attitude of the white man. There is no denying the strength of this argument. Personal observation has afforded many illustrations of both sides of the case.

An instance in point: A conservative Indian of New Mexico consented to dance a secular dance of his tribe; but he flatly refused to show the steps of a beautiful ceremonial dance. Nor would he for a long while give any reason for the refusal. At last, after much persuasion, he said, through an interpreter, "It is because you will tell *lies* about me." His fear—a fear that probably lurks in many another Indian heart—was evidently that he would be misrepresented at Washington.

Another instance: At an impressive Pueblo ceremonial the white folk who had been graciously allowed to attend were informed that it was not permitted to take photographs of this particular dance. Undaunted, several in the group levelled their cameras at the dancers. No fewer than five times did the Indian Governor of the Pueblo have to leave his post in the choir to remonstrate with the recalcitrant guests. "But I got four snap-shots all the same!" gleefully whispered one of the women to her companions.

Yet another instance: A curious, staring crowd of white men and women were gathered around a dignified chief, one of a group of Indians that had been taken on tour for a demonstration of Indian life and art. Suddenly one of the white women leaned forward and, in much the manner of a reporter interviewing a foreign visitor, said affably to the Indian chief: "And how do you like our country?" *Our* country!

Yes, lack of sympathy and of understanding on the part of the white race has, indeed, created obstacles to research. But not insuperable ones. Despite much of the Indian's experience with white folk—experience of their broken faith, of their misinterpretation of motive, of their assumption of lofty superiority as "discoverers" of America—the native good-will of the Red Man makes him still amenable to considerate treatment. Once convinced of the sincerity and friendliness and common sense of a white acquaintance, the patient aboriginal (man or woman) is generous in coöperation—as many students of Indian life can attest.

That the Indian's own attitude toward dancing is one of remarkable earnestness is manifest to the student at the outset. For example—

The Indian takes his dancing *disinterestedly*. He does not dance to earn his living; or to win applause on the stage—he is not working for curtain calls.

He takes his dancing *heroically*. And this, even to the point of self-sacrifice for a principle. "The Government may send its troops to shoot us down; but we will *not* cease our dancing," was the answer when the United States Government some years ago tried to put a stop to Indian ceremonies (as cited to the authors by Ernest Thompson Seton, who was present when the order was first issued to one of the tribes of the Southwest).

He takes his dancing *responsibly*. Night after night preceding a tribal ceremonial can the rumble of drum accompaniment be heard, making its way in sombre, muffled tones from the seclusion of the meeting-place where those chosen for the forthcoming performance are assembled. There, every step, every tone, every drum-beat, every syllable, is rehearsed diligently, lest there be a flaw of omission or commission in a ceremony designed to honor and propitiate, not offend, the spirit-powers.

And he takes his dancing *reverently*. Anyone who, like the present writers, has been granted the rare privilege of attending an all-night dance-ritual in a Pueblo Indian *kiva* (the sacred ceremonial underground chamber of secret tribal councils, devotions, and rehearsals, where commonly the profane foot of white man or woman dare not tread); anyone who has noted there the absorbed, the rapt, expression on the faces of the dancers; anyone who has felt there the rhythm of movement and song and inexorable drum-beat, that seems to make the hard ground throb with the throbbing of the dancers, and cry out with their cry that rain be sent to a thirsty land—anyone who has been responsive to all these things can but realize that in the dance the Indian finds a channel not only for the outlet of his esthetic nature but for the inflow of spiritual power.

Though in his own worship the white man has seen fit to retain other fine arts—music, poetry, painting, sculpture, architecture—he has lost the dance-art from the service of the church (except as it may be said to linger in the processional). For centuries he has been reading reverently in the Psalms the admonition: "Let them praise his name in the dance"; but he has left it to primitive man to give heed. Not left it, though, without some little interference; for civilization has been slow to perceive that every man must be permitted to approach the things of the spirit—whether of art or of religion—by the path that is familiar and beautiful to *his* feet.

Part Two

————————→ ⊛ ←————————

SOME CHARACTERISTIC
INDIAN DANCE STEPS

PART TWO

≻✵≺

BESIDES THE STEPS used in the complete dances or sections of dances described later, in Part Three, some characteristic Indian dance steps are herein analyzed. A few of these steps are compared, very briefly, with dance steps of some other races or nations; including that most highly developed and elaborate dance-art of the white race—the ballet, or "toe-dancing," of (notably) Italy, France, and Russia; and, through widespread adoption, of other European countries and the United States. The ballet form, in the niceties of its crystallized, traditional technique and of its exquisite though often artificial movements, probably offers the most striking contrast of all to the more natural expression of Indian dance-art—a case of the cultured *versus* the primitive. Since, owing to the limitations of the human frame, only a moderate number of movements are possible to it, whatever the race or the condition, there will, naturally, be found points of similarity even in these two extremes. And more especially so because of the fact that the orthodox ballet bears, in line, posture, and movement, unmistakable evidence that it too had its remote origin in a freer, more natural "out-door" style of dance—that of the ancient Greeks.

It is by no means the object, in this short, fragmentary treatise, to do more than barely touch on such comparisons and analogies; and that, merely by way of suggesting that this phase of the subject might possibly prove worthy of research in the future. The present brief—even hasty—excursion into so large and uncultivated a field can do no more than break ground at a single point. Even this slight jaunt, however, serves to show that Indian dancing is a distinctive and highly specialized form.

The three principal varieties of dancing have been concisely defined by Ethel L. Urlin (*Dancing, Ancient and Modern*) as: "(1) Dancing in which the legs are chiefly made use of, prevailing in Europe generally, and finding its most pronounced form in the orthodox ballet. (2) Dancing in which the arms and hands are chiefly used, carried to high perfection by the Javanese and also in Japan. (3) Dancing in which the muscles of the body play the chief part, as seen in Africa and Western Asia."

These elements are found also in combination in many dance-forms. In Spanish dancing, for example, arms, hands, head, torso, legs, and feet are strikingly in evidence; not to speak of very characteristic facial expression.

To none of the forms described does the dancing of the North American Indian, man or woman, seem specifically to belong. There are points of similarity, yes; but withal there is found in the dance-art of the Indian a mode that is peculiar to him. The chief element in the dancing of the tribes observed consists in foot and leg movements. Arm and hand movements are made in moderation, and at times are but a reflex action of the foot rhythms. The torso is for the greater part quiet, but relaxed. There is no change of facial expression. Exceptions to the foregoing generalizations were noted chiefly in the case of dances in which there is an element of dramatic impersonation; such, for example, as the wing-like motion of the arms in the Eagle Dance, or the realistic body movements in the burlesque "horse-tail" dance, or the plastic action of the Dog Dance.

In the tribes observed the men do the greater part of the dancing, though the women also often participate. In this respect the custom of the white race in modern times is reversed, at least in so far as the dance is considered in its use as a cultural and a dramatic art-form. In its social aspect—such as in the folk-dance and the ball-room dance of the white race—both sexes are equally represented. But in the dance in the schools and on the stage, girls and women now greatly preponderate, notwithstanding the late appearance—just two hundred and fifty years ago—of the female dancer in the European ballet. The Indian, in the importance he evidently attaches in his educational system to dancing by men, is but in line with some of the great nations and races of old—as witness, for example, the inclusion of dancing in the rigorous training that was given the stalwart Greek youths, that they might the better fulfill their part in the military, the religious, and the social scheme.

Since "the gesture of a people has a more ancient and unchanging history than its speech" (J. E. Crawford Flitch: *Modern Dancing and Dancers*), is it not conceivable that an exhaustive study of comparative dancing, with special reference to the art of the American Indian and other primitive races, might yield just as significant results as does the study of comparative philology?

* * * * *

For the purpose of conveying through the eye somewhat of the movement and posture of the Indian dancer, diagrams are given in the simple outline figures used in ballet directions—a "sign-language" familiar to students of dance-art. Now and then, for the sake of brevity or for lack of better words, terms relating to the orthodox ballet are employed in referring to some phases of Indian dancing. These terms, mostly in French or from the French, also form a sort of technical language among dance students—much as Italian terms are used by musicians, or Latin terms by the medical profession. The term "ballet" is herein used in its restricted sense as designating the form of dance-art commonly known as "toe-dancing"—not in its general sense as either a dance composition for stage performance or a corps of dancers in such a performance.

Some of the Indian steps given were observed in more than one tribe and in more than one kind of dance. The musical settings therefore differ with the various tribes or dances. This being the case, the steps are herein presented without special accompanying songs. Rhythm and speed play a large part, of course, in determining characteristic style and mood. Therefore in order to assist the student in forming an idea of the character of a given step, a simple rhythmic pattern and a metronomic indication of approximate speed are given when advisable. A more complete form of score—with tunes, words or syllables, drum-beat, and steps—is reserved for the dance examples in Part Three.

Indian dancing, like every other dance-form, can be reduced to a few basic movements. Besides the simplest form of *step*—such as is used in stepping forward or sidewise or backward—the basic Indian dance movements are the *jump*, the *hop*, the *skip*, and the *tap*. Since these terms are often used loosely or interchangeably in daily speech, they are herein, for the sake of clearness, restricted in meaning as follows:

Jump: a leap (a) from one foot to the other; or (b) on both feet simultaneously.

Hop: a short, brisk spring (a) on the ball of one foot; or (b) simultaneously on the toe of one foot and the ball of the other.

Skip: a step forward on one foot, followed immediately by a scraping or pushing or brushing movement of the same foot on the ground —designated brush-back, brush-forward, etc., as the case may be; then similar movements on the other foot; and so on.

Tap: a light touch, or pat, on the ground with either the ball or the toe of the foot.

(By the word *toe*, in Indian steps, is meant the part of the foot known in ballet parlance as the *half-toe*—not the point of the toe as in "toe-dancing.")

SPECIAL TERMS AND ABBREVIATIONS

In place: a step or steps made in one place—that is, without progressing forward, backward, or sidewise.

Flat: on the sole and heel of the foot.

Soft: relaxed, as opposed to tense, muscles.

Continue, with alternation: repetition of preceding movement, with alternating feet.

R: right.

L: left.

Ft: foot.

Forw: forward.

Side: sidewise.

A HIGHLY CHARACTERISTIC MOVEMENT

M.M. ♩=108 $\frac{2}{4}$

Jump on both feet

Jump on L ft; at same time raise R ft

Jump on both feet

Jump on R ft; at same time raise L ft

Continue, with alternation

The feet are parallel, and one foot is a few inches ahead of the other (see fig. 1 a). To make the step: (1) jump on both feet flat (see fig. 1 b); (2) jump on the left foot, holding the right foot up in front (see fig. 1 c); (3) jump on both

FIG. 1—A CHARACTERISTIC MOVEMENT

feet flat (see fig. 1 d); (4) jump on the right foot, holding the left foot up in front (see fig. 1 e); continue, with alternation.

Body and arm movements made with this step sometimes vary according to the fancy of the dancer. For example: some dancers exaggerate the movements, others move more calmly; some adopt a bending-forward posture (see fig. 1 a), others stand upright. The step may be done either in place or with a slight forward progression. It is sometimes done slowly, but commonly it is done rapidly.

The step is remarkably effective and gives the impression of exceeding lightness on the part of the dancer. To the observer it seems as if the feet touch the ground only for the purpose of springing away or rebounding from it. It is almost, indeed, as if the dancer's initial movement consisted in rising lightly *from* the ground as if from a spring-board, rather than in jumping *on* the ground. It is one of the most characteristic of the Indian dance steps observed. It is found in one or other of its forms in some war dances, as well as in dances of other types; such, for example, as the hoop dance of Taos Pueblo, and a "horse-tail" dance of Tesuque Pueblo that is said to be a burlesque of a Cheyenne dance.

The performance at Tesuque Pueblo of the last-mentioned—the "horse-tail," so to style it—was, by the way, an interesting example of the fact that the dignified Indian drops his reserve at times and manifestly enjoys his little joke. Each dancer's gay and elaborate costume included a horse-tail fastened to the belt in a way that enabled the wearer to operate it in truly comic fashion. The performance gave the impression of being a sort of go-as-you-please affair—not a set ceremonial. Indeed at times it seemed to have the spontaneity of improvisation. One dancer, for instance, rolled and squirmed on his back now and again; kicking up his legs the while like a fallen horse struggling to right itself—the kicks, by the way, were in perfect rhythm. Another varied his movements at intervals by dropping on his knees and quivering all over like a high-strung thoroughbred. Each dancer seemed to be interpreting the dance according to his own dramatic instinct. But for all the seeming impromptu, for all the prancing and kicking and wagging of tails, the unity of the whole as to rhythm and outline was not for a second marred.

Evidently the etiquette of the occasion demanded that the dancers go on dancing until the orchestra of drummers chose to stop drumming—and they did not choose to stop betimes! It was too good comedy to be cut short unduly. Time and again did the dancers come hopefully to a stop at what seemed a logical ending; only to be spurred on to further action by a fresh attack of the relentless drum-beat. The drummers were so convulsed with delight at the antics of the dancers that they kept on drumming until the spectators marvelled that the "horses" did not drop in their tracks from exhaustion.

An amplification of the characteristic step was noticed in the "horse-tail" dance, in addition to the original form. The first movement was the same —a jump on both feet. The second consisted of several quick jumps, instead of only one jump, on one foot (the free foot meanwhile being slightly advanced and the knee raised); followed by a repetition of these movements, with alternation. This variation is not unlike one of the figures of the Irish Jig. Oddly enough, the young Indian man who did the most brilliant dancing in the group—evidently a genius in the art—assumed with this step somewhat the same jaunty posture (hands on hips, elbows out, shoulders insolently forward) that is characteristic of the Irish Jig.

THE SKIP

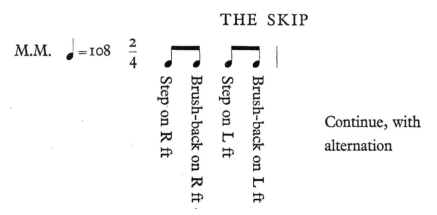

M.M. ♩ = 108   2/4

Step on R ft

Brush-back on R ft

Step on L ft

Brush-back on L ft

Continue, with alternation

The skip in some form is found nearly everywhere. A skip step that is common to Indian tribes consists of two movements: (1) a step on the ball of, say, the right foot—the weight is now on the right foot, and the left foot is off the ground; (2) a brush-back on the right foot; then continuation, with alternation. The second movement—the brush-back—is the reverse of that in the skip step common to the white races, in which there is a brush-*forward*, instead of a brush-*back*, movement. Though both the white and the Indian skipper *advance* in the course of the skipping, the brush-*back* movement of the Indian causes him to advance much more slowly than does the white skipper with his corresponding brush-*forward* step. The Indian skipper achieves his advancement by making the forward thrust of the foot (preparatory to the step) cover a greater distance than that covered by the brush-back movement. So he gets there in the long run.

The two modes of skipping differ too in the esthetic effect on the observer; and probably also in the emotional reaction of the performer. The skipping of white folk is more "springy": the Indian's is closer to the ground. The former expresses the care-free elation of youth: the latter suggests a more mature, cautious, subtle mood, a more suppressed excitement. It is probably the very deliberateness of the Indian skip step—the inch-by-inch progress, the advancing and retreating body—that creates in the observer a feeling of greater dramatic suspense, of more inexorable oncoming, than could ever be conveyed by swift and unretarded motion.

THE JUMP

Continuous jumping on both feet simultaneously seems common to many primitive races, including the Indian. Indian dancers seem able to jump on both feet—flat—without feeling the usual fatiguing effects of jarring movement; and this, notwithstanding that they often keep their dancing going for hours and hours at a time. The ballet dancer is trained to land on the ball of the foot, and with soft knee, in order to avoid jar. Even the most arduously trained male ballet dancers—such as those in the great Russian companies, with whom many amazingly difficult forms of the jump are a highly developed art—could not compete with such endurance as that of the Indian dancer. Relaxation of body in dance movements is, also, specially characteristic of primitive man. This is probably the reason why the Indian can keep up his dancing so much longer at a time than can the white dance artist.

A JUMP STEP
(Observed among Pueblo Indians)

M.M. ♩ = 104   2/4

Jump forw on L ft | Jump forw on R ft | Jump forw on L ft | Jump forw on R ft | Jump forw on L ft | Jump forw on R ft | Jump forw on L ft | Jump forw on R ft

The feet are parallel; but one foot, say the right, is about four inches farther forward than the other. The knees are soft. To make the step: stand on both feet; then (1) jump forward a few inches on the back foot, say the left; (2) jump forward quickly a few inches on the right foot, bringing it to the same distance ahead of the left foot that it was at the start. The movement gives a slow forward progress and has a peculiar, jerky effect. Both feet are kept close to the ground during the movement.

JUMPING ON BOTH FEET SIMULTANEOUSLY
(An Apache Devil-Dance Step)

The position is a low, squatting one, with both knees turned out. (See fig. 2 a.) The jumps are in even rhythm and close to the ground. They are made with both feet simultaneously, and flat for the greater part. At intervals the dancer stretches out one leg and taps the top of the toe on the ground; twisting leg and foot so as to turn the sole of the foot upward—not an easy feat by any means. Meanwhile there is a simultaneous jumping movement on the other foot. (See fig. 2 b.) These movements, from the Apache Devil Dance, are intentionally comic, grotesque; as are the costumes worn in the dance, which include black masks and huge head-dresses. The painted bodies of the dancers are nearly naked.

FIG. 2—APACHE DEVIL-DANCE STEP

A JUMP FROM ONE FOOT TO THE OTHER
(An Indian Counterpart of a Ballet *Jeté*)

One of the Indian jump steps may be compared to a ballet forward *jeté* (a leap from one foot to the other). To make the Indian jump: in preparation, stand on, say, the left foot, with the right knee relaxed, up, and *forward* (see fig. 3 a); then jump on the ball of the right foot, at the same time bringing the left knee up and forward; continue, with alternation. To make the ballet forward *jeté:* stand on, say, the left foot, with the right knee up and well turned *out,* the right foot arched, and the toe pointing downward (see fig. 3 b); leap on

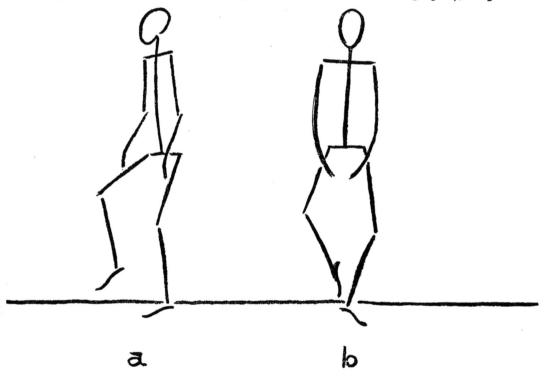

a   b

FIG. 3 — A JUMP FROM ONE FOOT TO THE OTHER
a, Indian; b, ballet

the ball of the right foot, and raise the left leg in the same position as that of the right leg in the beginning; continue, with alternation. The Indian movement, like the ballet, may be done one or more times in succession.

The relaxed condition and the natural position of the lifted foot of the Indian dancer in this step are the most striking points of contrast with the tense, stretched, turned-out foot and the downward-pointing toe so characteristic of the art of the ballet dancer.

A HOP STEP
(An Indian Counterpart of a Ballet *Sauté*)

To make the Indian hop step: stand on the ball of one foot, with the other raised either with a forward knee-lift (see fig. 4 a) or with a backward leg-extension (see fig. 4 b); then, in this position, hop one or more times on the ball of the former foot.

The principal difference between the Indian hop described and the ballet hop (*sauté*) is found in the contrast afforded by the less natural, though very beautiful, posture of the ballet form. The usual ballet *sauté* is done on the ball of one foot, say the right; with the left leg raised at the back and the toe of the left foot stretched. (See, for example, fig. 5 c.)

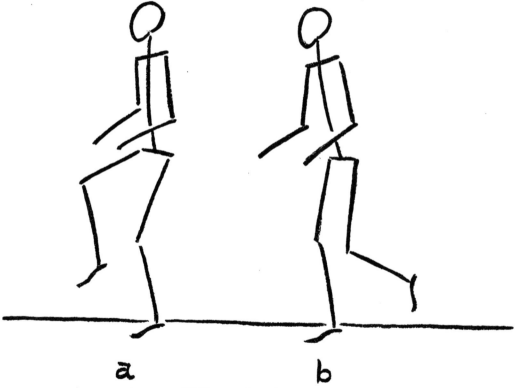

a   b

FIG. 4—A HOP STEP
a, forward position; b, backward position

A STEP FROM THE "SNOWBIRD" DANCE

(Observed at Tesuque Pueblo)

M.M. ♪=138 3/8

Jump forw onto R ft

Hop on R ft, keeping
L ft raised at back

Jump back onto L ft

Hop on L ft, keeping
R ft raised in front

Jump forw onto R ft

Hop on R ft, keeping
L ft raised at back

The step is one of the principal movements in the "Snowbird" Dance,—to call it, for convenience, by one of the many names by which it is popularly designated. Both men and women take part. The dancers form a large circle, men and women alternating in the line. Sometimes they face outward, sometimes inward; and diagonally toward the right. The men (each holding a bow and an arrow in the right hand and a rattle in the left) stand with feet parallel, but with the right foot about ten inches farther forward than the left foot—that is, the heel of the right foot is about as far forward as the toe of the left foot. Leaning over, they jump forward (a little toward the right) onto the right foot, and then hop on it; holding the raised left foot up at the back (see fig. 5 a). Next they jump back onto the left foot, and hop on it; holding the raised right foot up in front (see fig. 5 b). Since each jump toward the right covers more ground than the one back to the left, a slow progress around the circle is made.

The women are more moderate in their movements—Indian women are gentle, modest, retiring. Standing erect, and with feet side by side and parallel, they make two delicate little jumps to the right with both feet; then repeat the

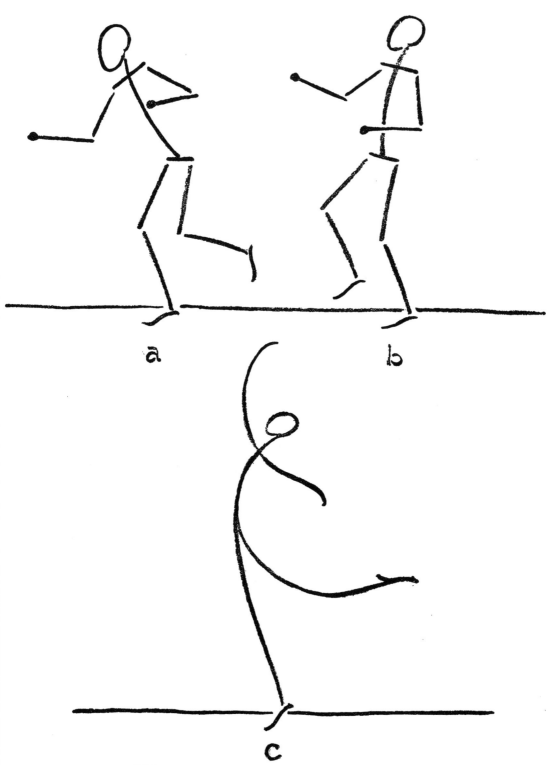

FIG. 5—A COMPARISON OF POSTURES

a, Indian; b, Indian; c, ballet

movement to the left. In their hands they hold little sprigs of evergreen (or sometimes eagle feathers), which, with a twist of the flexed forearm, they move from side to side in the rhythm of the steps. They wear their beautiful black hair falling straight and loose down their backs, and adorned with little feathery tufts like snowflakes—probably symbolic of fleecy rain-clouds.

A performance of the "Snowbird" Dance observed at Tesuque afforded an interesting illustration of how the execution of a composition, even when for group production, may differ in degree or style according to the personality or the conception of each individual interpreter. And this, without doing violence either to the prescribed form or to the ensemble effect. The movements of the long line of dancers ranged from the prim little steps of the women, through the energetic jumps of the majority of the men, to the splendid sweep and swing of a few specially ardent souls here and there among the men— temperamental artists who threw themselves into their work with fine fervor.

Movements similar to the principal step in the "Snowbird" Dance are found in some national dances and also in the ballet.

The ambition as well as the bane of the ballet student is to control the technique of "combinations"—that is, the combining of two or more steps into a phrase. For example: *jeté* and *sauté*—a leap from one foot to the other (*jeté*); then one or more hops on the latter foot (*sauté*). This is one of the simplest and easiest of the many ballet combinations. A charming Indian counterpart of a ballet *jeté-sauté* of this kind is the step of the men in the "Snowbird" Dance, already described.

The Indian *jeté-sauté*, so to style it, has of course its own characteristic posture—an intent bending-forward; presenting an interesting contrast to the buoyant posture in the ballet combination (see fig. 5 c).

A "COMANCHE" STEP

(Learned from a Group of Zuñi Girls)

M.M. ♩=84 2/4

Hop on L ft; at same time touch R toe to ground

Hop on L ft; at same time lift R ft toward back

Hop on L ft; at same time touch R toe to ground

Hop on L ft; at same time lift R ft toward back

Continue, *without* alternation

The dancers stand close together in single file. Each holds a rattle in the right hand, and has the left hand placed on the body below the chest. The left foot (on the ball) carries the weight. To make the step: (1) hop on the left foot, at the same time touching the right toe to the ground (see fig. 6 a); (2) hop on the left foot, at the same time lifting the right foot toward the back (see fig. 6 b). Continue, *without* alternation. In other words, there is a continuous hopping on the left foot; and with every *other* hop, a touch of the right toe to the ground.

The step is said to have been in a dance used to terrify Comanche enemies or prisoners in the olden time.

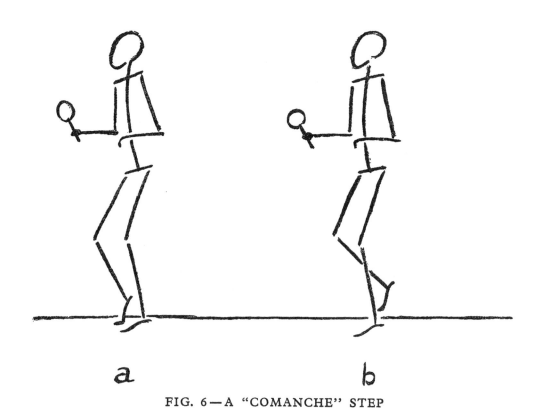

a   b

FIG. 6—A "COMANCHE" STEP

A TAP STEP

M.M. ♩=116   2/4   ♫ ♫ |

Tap on ball of R ft
Tap on ball of R ft
Tap on ball of L ft
Tap on ball of L ft

Continue, with
alternation

The position of the dancer in the tap step is the characteristic bending-forward one; with arms dangling. The movement may be made either in place or with slight forward progress. The taps are done twice in succession on each foot. With the second tap the weight is shifted to the tapping foot. The weight is on the outside of the ball of the foot; and the arch is, therefore, thrust up. The heel is raised, and the toe is slightly curled up so that it does not touch the ground. (See fig. 7 a.) Every tap is even and without jerkiness. To the civilized dancer the step seems simple; but the rapid tempo makes it difficult of execution. The foot at times seems almost as if glued to the ground, or as if impeded by a "stuttering" impulse.

Indian tapping is not strikingly like the tapping in the clog-dancing of the American Negro.

FIG. 7 — POSTURES IN THE TURN
a, Indian; b, Russian; c, Oriental

A TURN WITH TAPS

(Learned from an Indian from Tama, Iowa)

The turn in dance-art is widespread among the various races and nations. Especially is this true of the pivot-turn—a continuous revolving of the body in one direction by means of a movement of one foot aided by some sort of step by the other foot.

An Indian pivot-turn is made as follows: stand on the ball of one foot, say the left; then (1) tap the right foot; (2) tap the right foot again, and at the same time twist on the left foot around to the left. Thus a twist is made to the left with every other tap of the right foot, and the revolution is gradually completed. About sixteen taps are needed for each revolution. The bending-forward posture of the body, the outside ball-of-the-foot position, and the tempo are about the same as in the preceding tap step. (See fig. 7 a.)

The Indian pivot-turn described differs from many of the pivot-turns of other races in that the twisting foot of the Indian turn is kept on the ground and continuously carries the weight; whereas in other pivot-turns observed, each foot is lifted alternately.

A Russian pivot-turn (*national* Russian, not ballet) has a step on the ball of the back foot, instead of the tap of the Indian; and with it, characteristic arm positions are assumed. A Russian turn of this kind to the right is made as follows: Stand with the right foot flat. Place the left foot behind the right foot, with the left toe close to the heel of the right foot, and the left heel raised. Begin the turn by raising the right foot and stepping on it, flat, on the strong beat of the rhythm. (Often with this turn a brush-back is made by the left foot simultaneously with the step by the right foot.) Next, step on the ball of the left foot close to the right heel, at the same time lifting the right foot slightly off the ground. A continuous revolving is made with these steps. (See fig. 7 b.)

An Oriental pivot-turn resembles the preceding Russian turn, except that it, too, has its own characteristic arm position (see fig. 7 c).

The orthodox ballet has many kinds of turns—some of them very difficult and elaborate. The ballet turns are derived from two simple basic forms: (1) the turn which is made on the toes of both feet; and (2) that which is made on the toe of one foot only, in a rapid spinning movement. Both are strikingly unlike the Indian form.

A "TWO-STEP" OR WAR-DANCE STEP
(Learned from an Indian from Tama, Iowa)

M.M. ♩ = 104 $\frac{2}{4}$

Step side to R on R ft · *Close L ft to R ft* · *Step side to R on R ft* · *Close L ft to R ft*

Continue, without
change of direction

The knees are "soft." The movement progresses slowly sidewise, as follows: (1) step sidewise to, say, the right on the right foot; (2) bring the left foot to meet the right foot—that is, with the feet as near each other as in a normal standing position, a few inches apart (in ballet parlance this is to "step-close"); continue, without change of direction.

The Indian from whom this step was obtained called it both a "two-step" and a "war-dance step."

A similar step was made by a Sioux Indian, as follows:

M.M. ♩ = 104 $\frac{2}{4}$

Step in place on L ft · *Step side to R on R ft; at same time raise L knee* · *Close with L ft* · *Step side to R on R ft; at same time raise L knee*

Continue in
same direction

The Sioux began by making the first step on the foot that was not in the "line of direction" (as it is termed in the ballet)—that is, if the movement in this step is to be toward the right it is begun by the left foot; if the movement is to be toward the left it is begun by the right foot. For example: (1) step with, say, the left foot, in place, on the strong beat of the rhythm; (2) step sidewise to the right on the right foot, at the same time raising the left knee a little and thereby bringing the left foot slightly off the ground; (3) step on the left foot, closing to the right foot; (4) step sidewise to the right on the right foot, at the same time raising the left knee; continue in the same direction. This form of the step may be said rather to close and step than to step and close, since the left foot, say, closes on the strong beat, leaving the weak beat to the step by the right foot. The step on the left foot is in place only at the beginning; after which it closes toward the right foot.

A similar step is seen also in Spanish dancing. It is given with the characteristic click of the high heel. (The Indian, barefoot or with soft moccasins, has no boot heels to click.) In the Spanish form a step sidewise is made on one foot; then the other foot closes with a heel-tap, followed by a second heel-tap of the same foot; as follows:

$\frac{2}{4}$ — Step side to R on R ft — Tap L heel near R heel — Tap L heel slightly away from R heel — Step side to R on R ft — Tap L heel near R heel — Tap L heel slightly away from R heel

There is also a similar Russian step, with a brush-away movement; as follows:

$\frac{2}{4}$

Close L ft to R ft

Step side to R on R ft; at same time brush-away on L ft

Close L ft to R ft

Step side to R on R ft; at same time brush-away on L ft

AN INDIAN FORM OF THE *PAS DE BOURRÉE*
(Observed among Pueblo Indians)

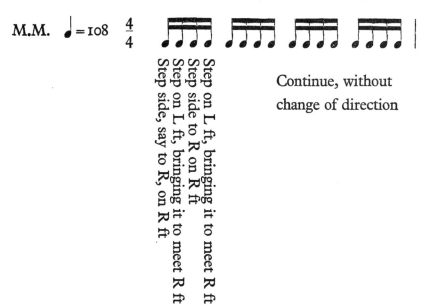

M.M. ♩ = 108

Step on L ft, bringing it to meet R ft
Step side to R on R ft
Step on L ft, bringing it to meet R ft
Step side, say to R, on R ft

Continue, without change of direction

For want of a better word, the ballet term, *pas de bourrée* (or "stuffing" step, so to speak), is here employed to designate the tiny steps on each foot—one following hard upon the other—found in both Indian and ballet dance-art.

In the ballet the toes are pointed outward and move in a crossed position (one foot close behind the other) in any desired direction. The knees are straight and tense. (See fig. 8 a.)

The Pueblo Indian does his *bourrée* with a difference. Though he, too, moves with tiny, rapid steps, he stands on the ball, not the toe, of each foot; his feet are parallel and side by side; his knees are soft; and he progresses sidewise only. His is altogether a more natural form. (See fig. 8 b.)

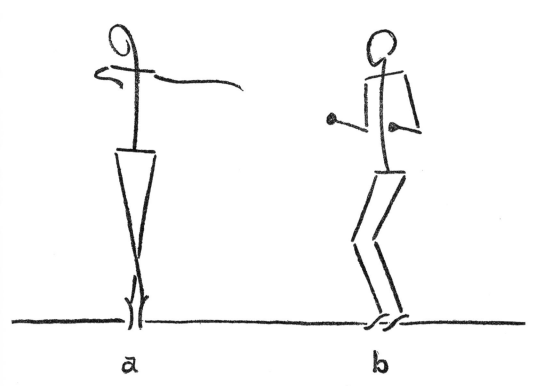

FIG. 8 — *PAS DE BOURRÉE*
a, ballet; b, Indian

A SIOUX STEP

(Obtained from a Sioux Indian)

M.M. ♩ = 80 2/4

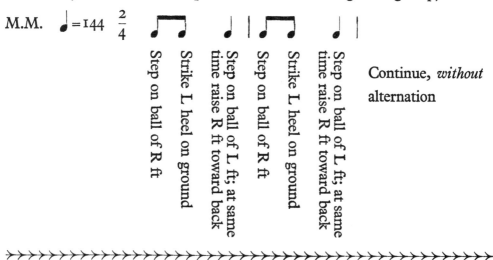

Step on ball of R ft · Lower R heel · Step on ball of L ft · Lower L heel

Continue, with alternation

The body is inclined forward; the head moves from side to side, in the rhythm of the beat; the knees are slightly bent. To make the foot-movements: (1) step forward a few inches on the ball of the right foot; (2) lower the right heel to the ground; continue, with alternation.

A HOPI STEP

(An Indian Counterpart of an American Negro Clog Step)

M.M. ♩ = 144 2/4

Step on ball of R ft · Strike L heel on ground · Step on ball of L ft; at same time raise R ft toward back · Step on ball of R ft · Strike L heel on ground · Step on ball of L ft; at same time raise R ft toward back

Continue, *without* alternation

‹‹‹

To make the movement: (1) step on the ball of the right foot; (2) strike the ground with the heel of the left foot, with the toe raised; (3) step on the ball of the left foot, heel up, and at the same time raise the right foot from the ground toward the back, preparatory to repeating the step; continue, *without* alternation.

The step is similar to a clog step of the American Negro.

In this connection it may be said that another Indian dance movement observed, done by a Jemez Indian, is strikingly suggestive of the Cake-walk of the American Negro. Of the Cake-walk, Ethel L. Urlin (*Dancing, Ancient and Modern*) has this to say: "It originated in Florida, where it is said that the Negroes borrowed the idea of it from the war dances of the Seminole. . . . The Negroes were present as spectators at these dances, which consisted of wild and hilarious jumping and gyrating, alternating with slow processions in which the dancers walked solemnly in couples. The idea grew, and style in walking came to be practiced among the Negroes as an art . . ." and "developed into the Cake-walk." On the other hand, Frederick W. Hodge, of the Museum of the American Indian, believes it more likely that the idea of the Cake-walk did not originate with the Seminole but in Africa, and may have been taken over by the Seminole from their Negro slaves.

‹‹‹

Part Three

EXAMPLES OF INDIAN DANCE
OF THE SOUTHWEST

PART THREE

————————————————————>⊛<————————————————————

THE CHOREOGRAPHY OF the six examples of Indian dance of the Southwest given herewith comprises movements, general directions, tunes, syllables, and drum-beat; or such of these as are called for by each composition. The steps are indicated in the score by reference-numbers.

The dance-song in Indian ceremonial is as inherent a part of the dance as the steps themselves. The tonality of the songs is often indeterminate. At times it seems to accord with familiar forms such as the diatonic or the pentatonic (five-tone) scale; then again it cannot, even by a great stretch of the imagination, be interpreted as conforming to any recognized mode. Some musicians claim that at times the Indians use an interval that is smaller than the semitone; but others believe that this effect is either a sliding of the voice, portamento, up or down to a given tone, or else a marked vibrato on the tone. Yet others think that it is simply a case of the singer's singing off the key— which has been known to happen to civilized singers! The portamento and an occasional and unintentional deviation from pitch would seem to explain many of the cases of intermediate sounds not expressible in terms of semitones.

The vocal tone used in the songs varies with the tribes. The tone of the Pueblo Indian women is light, high, gentle. That of many of the Pueblo Indian men is pitched low; and oftentimes it is almost inaudible—especially in song-endings. A rhythmic repetition or prolongation of vowel sounds gives a peculiar pulsating effect at times. The gypsy-like Navaho men, on the other hand, use either a high, squeezed, falsetto tone, or else a low quivering one, with the throat vibrating rapidly. Sometimes, too, it is like a short, sharp bark, as noted in the example given of a Navaho dance.

Some of the syllables of the songs make up specific words in poetic phrases; but many others are mere vocables that either never had any meaning, or else have come down from such remote periods that in the course of their long journey by word of mouth they have lost all semblance of meaning. The same fate, be it said, has overtaken the refrains of many of the old ballads and singing-games of the white man.

In some of the productions the dancers carry decorated gourd rattles; and oftentimes they wear strings of bells around their waists and knees, or jingle them in their hands. Usually these percussives merely react to the rhythm of body or foot movement; therefore it has not been necessary to indicate them in the scores.

Since rhythm plays so important a part in the life of the Indian it is natural that the drum—chief among rhythm-marking contrivances—should be the principal instrument of his orchestra. Often it is the only accompanying instrument. The drum is, indeed, the very heart-beat of Indian ceremonial. In the Southwest it is usually fashioned of the hollowed-out section of a cottonwood tree-trunk, with heavy skin stretched over top and bottom. A handle of thongs is attached to each rim. The Indian's love of beauty in color and design is effectively expressed in the decoration of the instrument. The tone, which is rich and sonorous, is produced by the percussion of a stick, used with loose wrist movement. The drumstick varies in form. A familiar kind terminates in a soft wadded knob like that of the usual kettle-drum stick. The typical Zuñi drumstick, which is believed by Frederick W. Hodge to be the oldest form, consists of a single slender strip of wood bent at one end into a circular, hoop-like head in such fashion as to make of it a highly resilient implement. In shape it somewhat resembles the figure 9. A stout string of skin binds the bent part of the strip securely in place where it joins.

Various kinds of drum-beat are employed, of which the following are often met with:

(*a*) A steady, even stroke; commonly unaccented.

(*b*) Groups of short tones—like triplets, for example; commonly unaccented.

(*c*) A tremolo.

(*d*) A single stroke, followed by a softer, lighter one that seems merely the reflex action of the stick after the rebound from its first impact with the drum-head. It is a highly characteristic form of Indian drum-beat. In the scores of the dances given herewith, this "rebound-beat" is indicated by an accented note connected by a slur with a note having a dot over it.

In place of the large drum, or even sometimes along with it, there are occasionally seen small percussive instruments on the order of a tambourine, but without the jingles. One variety consists of a wooden hoop covered at the top with stretched skin secured by thongs tied across the open end. In order not to dampen the tone by grasping the instrument by the hoop, tambourine-fashion, the player holds it by the thongs. The tone is produced by the stroke of a small stick with wadded knob. "We call the little drum 'teh-teh,'" said a Tewa Indian, forming an onomatopœic word that suggested the sound of a light rat-tat on a drum.

The "teh-teh," so to style it, not only figures in some of the dance productions but is often used instead of the big, heavy drum by the old men in teaching the little children to dance and sing. The American Indian literally absorbs rhythm from babyhood—it seems that the babies are even deliberately coddled rhythmically. Apt pupils, therefore, are the young folk, who in their fine rhythmic response could put to shame many a civilized dance or music student.

Thus is the little Indian initiated betimes into the intricacies of native song and movement. Thus is he made ready to carry on worthily the sacred tradition of tribal rite and ceremony. And thus does he make glad the hearts of the grandsires in their labor of love and loyalty.

* * * * *

N. B. A dash (–) after a syllable in the word-parts of the scores indicates a continuation of the vowel sound with which the syllable ends, through the time-value of the note over the dash; carrying with it, however, a distinct, separate pulsation of the voice.

Since the tribes represented in the dance examples have no written language the pronunciation of the words and vocables in the scores is indicated phonetically. The consonants are to be pronounced about as in English; the vowels *a, e, i, o,* about as in most European languages; but the vowel *u,* for the sake of clearness, is rendered *oo.* The digraph *ch* is to be pronounced as in *child.*

Unless otherwise specified, foot placement or body position indicated by a reference-number under a given note or rest is to be held until the next reference-number—that is, through any intervening notes or rests that are not numbered.

Slight variations in the rendering of parts of the dances—in both steps and music—were noticed at different times. Some of these are indicated in the scores by time-signatures in parentheses and vertical dotted lines for bars dividing measures. The versions given herewith seemed the most typical of the interpretations noted.

≺≺≺

EAGLE DANCE

To the Indian, a bird soaring aloft or a feather wafted up by the breeze is, in its lightness of ascent and its ethereal beauty, exquisitely symbolic as a carrier of prayer from the heart of man to the ears of the gods. The eagle—most majestic of birds—is therefore an object of special veneration. It is the sacred bird—the Thunder Bird. In the arid regions of the Pueblos great numbers of songs and ceremonies are virtually prayers for rain; and the dance that embodies the Thunder Bird is naturally one of the most widely known ceremonies among the Pueblo tribes. And, too, it is one of the most realistic of those of their dances that take the form of dramatic impersonation.

There are various versions concerning the origin and meaning of the Eagle Dance. One of these is that it is part of an ancient ceremony relating to the rain and the crops. It is told also that the eagle was once sent over Pueblos that had been stricken with a plague. The Thunder Bird started the wind blowing; whereupon rain-clouds formed, and the rain fell and wiped away the plague. The Eagle Dance is thought to be a fragment of an old ceremonial that commemorated this divine mercy.

The dance varies in different Pueblo tribes; but its general effect is the same in all. Similar steps are used, but not always in the same order. The music varies. There are differences in tempo. The hopping portion of the dance, for example, is presented at much greater speed by some tribes than by others. At San Ildefonso Pueblo there are two sets of songs, used on different occasions, that show variations in the order of the steps. The form herewith presented, learned from a San Ildefonso Indian, is the more effective of these two versions.

With the exception of the entrance part (Song I), the tunes of the Eagle Dance were transcribed by Dr. George Herzog, of the University of Chicago.

≺≺≺

The dance is usually performed by two men; one representing the male, and the other the female bird. They imitate the movements of the eagle—stepping, hopping, soaring, alighting, mating. In appearance they show equal fidelity to nature. Their naked bodies and legs are realistically painted. A very short skirt is worn; also a close-fitting, cap-like headgear, terminating in front in a long beak. Great feather wings are fastened to the arms of each dancer. The feathers are attached to a single strip of material a few inches wide, and long enough to extend from the fingers of one hand across the back to the fingers of the other hand. At each end there is a loop for the hand to grasp; and in the middle there is a cord to tie around the neck. The winged arms of each dancer are outstretched throughout the dance, and they rotate as if on pivots, without elbow bend. A feather tail is fastened to the belt at the back.

First Song. This song serves merely for the entrance and the exit of the dancers. In each case they are accompanied (musically, as well as processionally and recessionally) by a choir of singers and drummers. The musicians follow the dancers during the entrance and the exit measures, but stand in one place during the dance proper. The song is repeated as many times as may be necessary in order for the dancers to reach the spot whereon they are to give the dance. Throughout the entrance and the exit measures the dancers maintain a semi-squatting posture to represent a bird (see fig. 9 a).

The step of the song (an easy one) consists of a slow, progressive motion made by putting on the ground the ball of one foot and then lowering to the ground the heel of the same foot; and a continuation, with alternation. *Each* of these two foot movements—that is, the one of the ball and the one of the heel—has the value of one quarter-note. With each, the knee is thrust forward a little, giving the steps a springy, bird-like aspect. One dancer follows the other.

The advent of the dancers is sometimes heralded by a tremolo on the drum; merging, on their appearance, into the first song. This rumbling tremolo overture is occasionally heard preceding other dances also. Whether or not it is intended as a touch of realism in the Eagle Dance, it certainly proves a highly suggestive announcement of the coming of the Thunder Birds. The "eagles" make their entrance upon the scene with fine dignity and aloofness, and consistently maintain the mood throughout the ceremony. From the very beginning the interpretation appeals powerfully to the imagination of the beholder.

Second Song. The dance proper begins with the second song, in which the two dancers progress very slowly. At times they move in large circles, one dancer following the other; at other times they move in small individual circles. With the exception of a slight shifting of the rhythmic stepping at a certain point (indicated in the score) the step is the same as in the first song. The dancers continue in a semi-squatting posture.

Third Song. The dancers are still in a semi-squatting posture; and in certain measures (indicated in the score) they squat close to the ground (see fig. 9 b). Instead of the ball-and-heel movements of the first two songs, the steps of the third song are on the ball of the foot. In some measures the dancers move with slow steps, off the regular beat of the music. Their wings rotate in larger circles than hitherto.

Fourth Song. In this song the tune of the third song is repeated; but since in other respects it practically amounts to a fourth part, it is so treated here for the sake of clearness. Changes in tempo, drum-beat, and steps give it a distinctive character notwithstanding its unchanged melody. The speed throughout the greater part of the song is increased—in some Pueblos it is almost doubled.

The step consists of a hop sidewise on both feet simultaneously; with one foot on the ball and the other on the toe. In the hop to the right, for example, the left foot is on the ball and carries the weight, and the toe of the right foot touches the ground; in the hop to the left the right foot is on the ball and carries the weight, and the toe of the left foot touches the ground. The body is inclined "in opposition" to the step—that is, the body leans in the opposite direction from that toward which the step is made. The knees are no longer bent in a squatting position. (See fig. 9 c.) The movement is made, with alternation, as follows:

Measures 1–4: the hops are to the right; the body is inclined to the left. Measures 5–10: the hops are to the left; the body is inclined to the right. Measures 11–13: the hops are to the right; the body is inclined to the left. The dancers, with their brisk staccato movements, have an astonishingly bird-like mien in this part.

FIG. 9—EAGLE DANCE
a, semi-squat; b, low squat; c, hopping position

EAGLE DANCE

(Original Sung in Lower Key)

Song I (for Entrance and Exit)

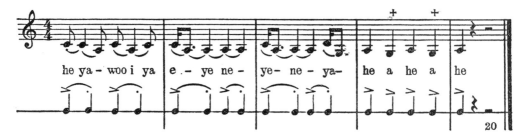

EAGLE DANCE—Continued

Song III

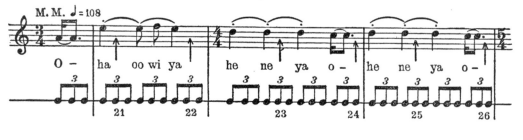

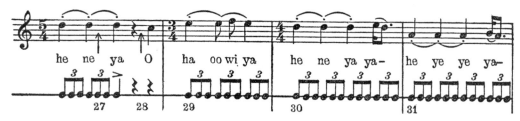

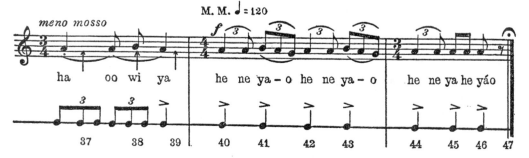

EAGLE DANCE—Continued

Song IV

O - ha oo wi ya he ne ya o - he ne ya o -

48 49 50 51

he ne ya O ha oo wi ya he ne ya ya- he ye ye ya-

52 53 54 55 56

he ne ya - o - he ne ya - o - he ne ya O -

57 58

meno mosso   *stringendo*

ha oo wi ya he ne ya - o he ne ya - o he ne ya he yáo

59 60 61 62 63 64 65 66 67 68

(Explanation of step reference-numbers in score.)

EAGLE DANCE

Song I

(Drum tremolo *ad libitum* preceding first appearance of dancers.)

1. Step on ball of right foot.
2. Lower right heel.
3. Step on ball of left foot.
4. Lower left heel.

Continue, to end of song, regular stepping movements 1–4 as in first two measures. Throughout Song I and Song II the posture is a semi-squat.

Song II

5. Continue to hold last step of Song I.
6. Step on ball of right foot.
7. Lower right heel.
8. Step on ball of left foot.
9. Lower left heel.
10. Step on ball of right foot.
11. Lower right heel.
12. Hold position and bend right knee; bend body to right; right wing near ground.
13. Move body back to original position; touch ball of left foot to ground.
14. Keep both feet on ground as in number 13, but thrust knees forward.
15. Lower left heel.
16. Step on ball of right foot.

17. Lower right heel.
18. Step on ball of left foot.
19. Lower left heel.

Continue regular stepping movements, with alternation, to last measure of song. End the step with the weight on the left foot.

20. Hold position over to first step (21) in next song.

Song III

21. Step on ball of right foot.
22. Step on ball of left foot.
23. Step on ball of right foot.
24. Step on ball of left foot.
25. Step on ball of right foot.
26. Step on ball of left foot.
27. Step on ball of right foot.
28. Step on ball of left foot.

The position of the foregoing eight steps (21–28) in relation to the tune is indicated in the score by arrow-heads. The steps are evenly distributed. The body posture in these steps (21–28) is a semi-squat, as in Songs I and II.

29. Squat very low.
30. Twist body to right, and look on ground to right.
31. Remain in squatting position, but twist body to left, and look on ground to left.
32. Rise gradually during measure to original semi-squatting position as at beginning of song.

33. Step on ball of right foot.

34. Step on ball of left foot.

35. Step on ball of right foot.

36. Step on ball of left foot. The right foot, which has been lifted naturally in preparation for its next step, remains off the ground until needed for the step (37) in next measure.

37. Step on ball of right foot.

38. Step on ball of left foot.

39. Step on ball of right foot.

40. Step on ball of left foot.

41. Step on ball of right foot.

42. Step on ball of left foot.

43. Step on ball of right foot.

44. Step on ball of left foot.

45. Step on ball of right foot.

46. Squat low, with weight on both feet.

47. Pause, and begin to rise.

Song IV

48. Complete the rising movement. The posture is no longer a squatting one.

In the following hopping movements the feet when on the ground are in these positions: In hops to the right, the left foot is on the ball and carries the weight, and the toe of the right foot touches the ground. In hops to the left, the foregoing is reversed. The hops are made on both feet simultaneously.

49. Hop on both feet to right.

50. Hop on both feet to right.

51. Hop on both feet to right.

> Continue hopping on both feet to right on each beat through 52.

52. After the hop on this beat, hold position through quarter-rest.
53. Shift weight to right foot in preparation for hops to left.
54. Hop on both feet to left.
55. Hop on both feet to left.
56. Hop on both feet to left.

> Continue hopping on both feet to left on each beat through 57.

57. After the hop on this beat, hold position through quarter-rest.
58. Shift weight to left foot in preparation for hops to right.
59, 60, 61, 62, 63, 64, 65, 66, 67, and 68. Hop on both feet to right on each beat (a hop to each number).

Exit: Song I.

N. B. Notes in parentheses are sung with less intensity than ordinarily. A cross above a note indicates about a quarter-tone higher.

‹‹

WAR DANCE

Steps and music of Indian war dances vary of course among the tribes. The form here given was learned from a Tewa Indian in New Mexico, but a similar step has been observed in other places also. There are two sections in the example here referred to, of which the first is given. The second is very much like the first, but in it both music and steps greatly increase the speed. Variation in the rendering of several measures of the tune, due probably to the singer's unconscious deviation from the original pitch and time, was noticed on different occasions. Entire accuracy in the recording is not, therefore, claimed; but the version presented herewith seemed the most typical of the forms heard. In one rendering, the singer dropped an octave below the notes of the closing two measures—probably because his deep voice felt more comfortable down there.

The body position in the dance is the usual bending-forward one. An arrow or a tomahawk is held in the right hand and a feather in the left. The elbows are flexed and the hands held forward. The dancers turn their heads to look from side to side, in rhythm with the foot movements. To make the step: (1) touch the ball of the right foot to the ground about a foot-length forward; (2) slide the right foot back a few inches and shift the weight to it, with the heel lowered to the ground; continue, with alternation. The dance is repeated many times.

This characteristic movement is most primitive and effective, with the crouching body, the stealthy step, the furtive glance from side to side—all vividly suggesting expectancy of a lurking enemy.

‹‹

WAR DANCE

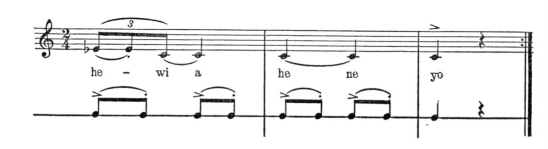

(Explanation of step reference-numbers in score.)

WAR DANCE

1. Touch ball of right foot on ground, about a foot-length forward.
2. Slide right foot back a few inches, shifting the weight to it as the heel is lowered.
3. Touch ball of left foot on ground, about a foot-length forward.
4. Slide left foot back a few inches, shifting the weight to it as the heel is lowered.

Continue movements 1–4 to end, with same time-value. Turn the head and look to right when ball of right foot is touched forward; and turn the head and look to left when ball of left foot is touched forward.

SUN DANCE
(Learned from a San Ildefonso Indian)

The Sun Dance celebrates the return of Spring and the planting and growth of the corn under the kindly sun. Four persons perform the dance. They stand in single file, about two feet apart. Each holds a rattle in the right hand, which is shaken slightly at each step of the right foot. A bow and an arrow are held in the left hand. Once in the course of the dance the dancers face about; before the end they turn again to the original position. The movements are practically all in place—a characteristic of many Indian dances. There are no difficult steps; and, with the exception of a series of little hops on both feet at certain times and of taps with one foot at other times, the movement is the same throughout. In the principal movement (designated hereinafter the "main-step") every step on the right foot is made with marked emphasis. The elbows are flexed.

To make the main-step: (1) take a step in place on the right foot, flat, and simultaneously raise the left heel high, but without lifting the toe from the ground (see fig. 10 a)—some specially energetic dancers, however, raise the whole left foot slightly off the ground, instead of only the heel; (2) lower the left heel, and at the same time raise the right foot in preparation for continuing the step. In the main-step both knees are bent slightly, the left more than the right.

In the hopping step already referred to, which occurs in B, the body, when the hop is made to the right, is inclined backward to the left, but with a slight twist to the right; the head is thrown slightly back, but faces right. The left foot is on the ball and carries the weight, and the left knee is slightly bent. The toe end of the right foot is on the ground, with the right heel raised. Both arms are stretched out to the right. (See fig. 10 b.) The foregoing is reversed when the hop is to the left. Similar body positions are assumed when the groups of taps are made with the right foot, as indicated in the score; and with the taps, the hands are given a slight impulse with the accent of the rhythm. The dance changes frequently in time and tempo.

The tunes were transcribed by Dr. George Herzog.

SUN DANCE
(Original Sung a Fifth Lower)

SUN DANCE—Continued

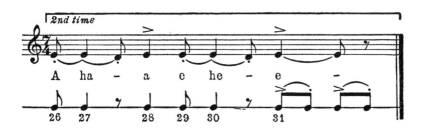

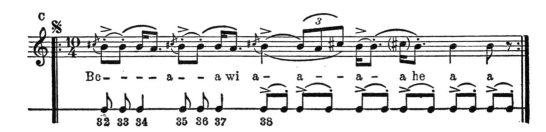

SUN DANCE—Continued

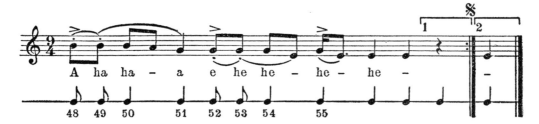

(Explanation of step reference-numbers in score.)

SUN DANCE

(The dance is done practically in place)

A

1. Step on right foot flat; at same time raise left heel.
2. Lower left heel; at same time raise right foot.

Movements 1 and 2 comprise the "main-step." For more detailed directions see previous description of the Sun Dance.

Continue main-step to end of section, without alternation.

FIG. 10 — SUN DANCE

Note that in this section each of the two movements—1 and 2—of the main-step has the value of an 8th-note, coinciding with the drum-beat value.

B

3. Step on right foot flat; at same time raise left heel.
4. Lower left heel; at same time raise right foot.
5 and 6. The same as 3 and 4.
7 and 8. The same as 3 and 4.

Note that in numbers 3–8 the main-step is continued but that each of its two movements has the value of a quarter-note, coinciding with the drum-beat value.

9. Step on right foot flat; at same time raise left heel.
10. Lower left heel; at same time raise right foot.
11 and 12. The same as 9 and 10.
13 and 14. The same as 9 and 10.

Note that in numbers 9–14 the main-step is continued but that each of its two movements has the value of an 8th-note as in A, coinciding with the drum-beat value.

15. Main-step throughout measure as in preceding measure, coinciding with the drum-beat values.
16. Main-step throughout measure, each movement in 8th-note value.
17. The main-step on this last beat of the measure is continued in 8th-note values, *not* coinciding with the quarter-note value of the drum-beat.
18. Preparation: Body inclined to left, but twisted to right; legs and feet still in front position; both arms up to right; right heel off ground.

First time:

19, 20, and 21. Hop three times a few inches to right on both feet (a hop to each number). The ball of the left foot carries the weight; the right toe touches the ground.

22, 23, and 24. Hop three times a few inches to left on both feet; body inclined to right, but twisted to left; legs remain forward; arms up to left. The ball of the right foot carries the weight; the left toe touches the ground.

25. Main-step to end of measure, coinciding with the drum-beat value; facing front.

Second time:

26, 27, and 28. Hop three times to right on both feet as in 19–21; body inclined to left, but twisted to right; arms up to right.

29 and 30. Hop twice to left on both feet as in 22–23; body inclined to right, but twisted to left; arms up to left.

31. Main-step to end of measure, coinciding with the drum-beat value; facing front.

C

32, 33, and 34. Tap right foot three times (a tap to each number); with each tap, strike out arms up to right; body and head twisted to right.

35, 36, and 37. Tap right foot three times; reverse to left the other movements and positions of the preceding numbers (32–34).

38. Main-step to end of measure, coinciding with the drum-beat value; facing front.

D

39, 40, 41, 42, and 43. Tap right foot five times; with each tap, strike right arm up forward; body and head facing front.

44. Tap right foot; with tap, strike out arms up to right; body and head twisted to right.

45. Repeat preceding (44).

46. Tap right foot; reverse to left the other movements and positions of number 44.

47. Main-step to end of measure, in 8th-note values, *not* coinciding with the quarter-note value of each drum-beat; facing front.

48, 49, 50, and 51. Tap right foot four times; with each tap, strike out arms up to right; body and head twisted to right.

52, 53, and 54. Tap right foot three times; reverse to left the other movements and positions of the preceding numbers (48-51).

55. Main-step to end of measure, in 8th-note values, *not* coinciding with the quarter-note value of each drum-beat; facing front.

Repeat C and D in full, closing with the second ending.

E

56. Tap right foot; with tap, strike right arm up forward; body and head facing front.

57. Draw right arm back to body.

58. Tap right foot; with tap, strike right arm up forward; body and head still facing front.

59. Repeat preceding (58).

60. Draw right arm back to body.

61, 62, and 63. Tap right foot three times; with each tap, strike right arm up forward; body and head still facing front.

64, 65, 66, and 67. Tap right foot four times; with each tap, strike out arms up to right; body and head twisted to right.

68, 69, and 70. Tap right foot three times; reverse to left the other movements and positions of the preceding numbers (64–67).

71. Main-step to end, in 8th-note values, *not* coinciding with the quarter-note value of each drum-beat; facing front.

N. B. Notes in parentheses are sung with less intensity than ordinarily.

A cross above a note indicates about a quarter-tone higher.

Singers and a drummer accompany the dancers.

MATACHINES

(Learned from a San Ildefonso Indian)

The Matachines (*Los Matachines* in the Spanish, and usually called *Matachina* by the Indians) is a curious and puzzling example of mixed influences. In nearly every other Indian ceremony observed by the authors the make-up, or component parts, of the dance proper—*steps, music, instruments, costume, meaning*—seemed distinctively, characteristically *Indian*. Such customary and admirable consistency in no wise marks the productions of the Matachines. For example:

(*a*) The *steps* (to be analyzed later) are unlike any other Indian movements observed.

(*b*) The *music*, for the greater part, is more like happy little European folk-tunes than Indian melodies. The actual origin of the tunes is not definitely known—at least to the present writers.

(*c*) The *instrument* usually giving out the tunes is no Indian product—it is a violin, played by a Mexican fiddler. There is no voice-part.

(*d*) The *costume* of the principal dancers—the Matachines proper—well-nigh defies description. At San Ildefonso, for example, it usually consists of long, wide white trousers; a fringed Spanish shawl over a shirt or a coat; a mask consisting of a scarf drawn across the lower part of the face and a strip of black bead fringe falling over the upper part of the face; a little rattle concealed in a bright scarf and held in the right hand; a decorated wooden trident held in the left hand; and, topping off the whole, by way of headgear a bishop's mitre that sparkles with ornaments and culminates at the apex in a cross. Long streamers of brightly colored ribbons are attached to the mitre and float gayly in the breeze with the movement of the dancer. (It should be said here that other forms of headdress, more Indian in character, are used in some places in the Matachines, and ancient specimens are preserved in museum collections. The customary headgear is, however, unmistakably a *mitre* in appearance.) One of the Matachines (called *Mananca*) acts as their leader. He wears, instead of a mitre, a cap-like crown surmounted by a little cross. Besides the group of Matachines thus costumed, several other performers participate in the dance. One of these is an unsmiling little Indian girl (called *Malinche*) in white frock, clumsy black leather "store" shoes, and long white net veil held in place by a wreath of white artificial flowers—looking for all the world like a demure young candidate about to make her first communion. Two mimes—one, a boy wearing the hide and the head of a bull; the other, a man presenting an exaggeratedly patriarchal appearance and armed with a whip and a wooden knife—complete the group. The costumes of the performers vary somewhat among the tribes.

(*e*) And finally, the *origin*, the *meaning!* Alas, that is as perplexing, as obscure, as the dance elements. Numerous conflicting theories and legends have woven themselves around the Matachines. Here are a few of them, given at random:

It is derived from a beautiful old religious ceremonial of southern Europe. It is found in Persia. It celebrates the conversion of the Indians to Christianity. It is the Indian version of the age-old, symbolic conflict between good and evil, with the ultimate victory of the good. It represents the warfare against sin that began after the Resurrection. The little girl typifies the Church; she is pursued by Sin and the Devil, but escapes from them; and she rescues the people, as the Church rescues those in its fold. The two grotesque mimes personify Sin and Death; they are at war with, and are finally destroyed by, the Church, or by each other. It represents a Mexican bull-fight. It is an old comic dance, with a mock fight, that was once well known in France and Italy. It is a Mexican dance. It came from Montezuma, last ruler of the Aztecs. It is of Moorish origin and was brought over by the Spaniards. And so it goes.

Most picturesque of these multifarious versions are those that embody myths and legends of Montezuma. In these stories the girl in the drama is often identified with the Indian woman of Mexico, the beloved of Cortés—Marina, or Malintzin, or Malinche, who acted as interpreter and intermediary between the Spaniards and the Aztecs in the affairs of the Conquest. In the legends of the Matachines she appears variously: as the favorite of Cortés; as the wife of Cortés; as the wife of Montezuma; as the daughter of Montezuma. Mananca, leader of the Matachines, is called in some places *El Monarca*, the monarch. He is identified with the Pueblo Indian father, Poseyémo; and, through further myth-accretion, also with Montezuma.

The story of the pantomime told by the Cochiti Indians is narrated by Paul A. F. Walter in *Art and Archaeology*, vol. ix, 1920, as follows: "The Princess Malinche, given in marriage to Cortés by Montezuma, fell under the influence of El Toro (the Bull), Spirit of Malevolence, and at the behest of Cortés persuaded her father to desert his people, the Aztecs. Her grandfather (El Abuelo) vainly pleads with her and is finally slain by El Toro after a spirited contest. However, the grandfather, as a Koshare (ancestral spirit), returns from the land of the ancients, and his promptings work a change of heart in Malinche, who leads Montezuma back to his people."

Interesting material was obtained for the authors by Helen H. Roberts, of Yale University, who is doing research work in music among the Indians. Miss Roberts states: "An Indian from Taos and one from San Ildefonso both say, without knowledge of one another's information, that the Matachina dance came from Montezuma, when he journeyed through the country before the coming of the Spaniards. These Indians say also that Montezuma prophesied that the Spaniards and the Americans would some day be all around them. 'The Taos people,' I was told by the Taos Indian, 'have no masked dance except the Matachina, which they got from Montezuma, when he came up the Rio Grande many years ago. He gave them the songs and now they copy them with a violin.'

"The Matachina dance," Miss Roberts says further, "is given at Christmas at Santa Clara Pueblo. To quote the words of my Indian informant there: 'The Santa Clara people got the Matachina dance from an old man at San Juan. Up there, though, they have a Mexican play the violin, but not at Santa Clara. I think the old man made it up. He is dead now. Oseyémo [Poseyémo?] is the name of the old Indian father. I think he danced that dance, for it is an Oseyémo dance. Oseyémo used to live up at El Rito. He was a great father of all the Indians. From up there he went to Old Mexico and there is where he live. He is just like a spirit. He would come up every June 24 and go to El Rito to see his mother. She is a spirit too. The Indians might see him but they don't know him. He is dressed and looks like a Mexican, got boots and spurs and rides horseback.' " †

The Indian from whom the dance steps were learned, when asked concerning the origin of the Matachines, said: "It is the Montezuma's first dance." And he added: "I don't know just what it mean." Sensible Indian!

As to the Moorish origin of the Matachines, the name itself is not without suggestiveness. The Spanish word *matachin* (plural, *matachines*) is defined variously as (1) a buffoon; (2) a grotesque masked dance or a performer in the dance; (3) a butcher, a slaughterman. Any or all of these terms, by the way, may well be applied to the Indian form of the dance. And the theory that traces its origin to the Moors (the Arabic conquerors of Spain) is given weight by the fact that according to etymologists the Spanish *matachin* is derived from *motawajjihn* or *mutawajjihin*, an Arabic word meaning *maskers* or *assuming masks*.

But, be it said—whether the prototype of this bizarre product is Moorish or Spanish; Aztec or Pueblo; pagan or Christian; a farce or a tragedy; a bull-fight or a sacred symbol; or is compounded of all—the artistic North American aborigines have somehow succeeded in blending the whole into an engrossing ceremony.

*   *   *   *   *

At San Ildefonso, Matachines is a Christmas Day celebration. The Indians there begin the holy day by going to Mass; and they continue their observance by dancing Matachines out-of-doors in the morning and again in the afternoon, with a pause for the midday meal. The ceremony is begun with dancing by the mitred men, the Matachines, who continue in movement throughout the performance. Led by Mananca, they stand in two lines in single file and face forward the greater part of the time. At one end of the lines sit the Mexican musicians, who provide the violin, or violin and guitar, accompaniment. Later on, the grandfather and the little girl participate actively. Finally comes the pugnacious bull—whereupon fearsome combat and slaughter ensue. Though in the heat of conflict the grandfather and the bull carry on vigorously between the lines, never do they for a moment disturb the rhythm or the alignment of the imperturbable Matachines, who proceed aloofly with their strange dance. And up and down between the lines the solemn child in bridal white moves rhythmically. Shouts of laughter from Indian and Mexican onlookers greet the mimes. Even the mitred dancers can ill conceal, behind their fringe masks, eyes that now and again gleam with mirth at the goings-on of the old man and the bull. At the close of the dance, after the killing of the bull, the Matachines kneel.

Though the rôles of the grandfather (*El Abuelo*) and the bull (*El Toro*) present a fairly obvious and familiar style of comedy characterization, the Indian's impersonation of a *matachin*, on the other hand, is so different and peculiar an interpretation that the effect of the performance as a whole is almost as if two distinct dance-dramas were being enacted side by side by two groups of performers, each group taking little or no cognizance of the other.

The following description—given in the words of a San Ildefonso Indian woman (Tan-ta), in response to queries by the authors—affords a graphic, first-hand "scenario" of the production:

"The men dance on each side as many as the Governor said, sometime five or six. Mananca is the leader of the dancers in the middle. Mananca wears the same kind of clothes. He has a crown. Sometime he sit down at one end. He's the leader. He dance and the others dancers dance and do just what Mananca do. The little girl dress in white belong to the dance too. She use the same steps as the other dancers all the time till is over. The girl don't do anything else but dance. The girl follow Mananca and dance just like him. Old grandfather he says all kinds of funny things to the people and they laugh. Sometime he is call Abuelo, but it is Mexican word. We call him old grandfather. He watch the dancers to see if they do it right. If not, he whip them. If the little girl don't know how to do, grandfather leads her. He hold her and show her how to do. The bull scare the people. He run after them, but he fight with the grandfather more. In some parts grandfather and bull use dance steps and some parts they do funny things to make the people laughed. The bull make the old grandfather mad. The girl also make the bull mad and the grandfather help her. The girl has a handkerchief, and while the bull come in the middle the girl throw the handkerchief at him and scare the bull. The bull kick grandfather and throw dirt on him. The grandfather throw a rope on him and catch him and kill him. Sometime grandfather sit down on the chair on one end, the other end from the Mexicans playing the music—before he kill the bull. The bull is in the dance just till they throw him down and kill him. Grandfather play that he kill the bull and cut him and throw the meat to the people. Then they takes him away. The Governor takes the bull away. The little girl and grandfather dance till the dance is over. At the last part, after the bull is taken away, the Matachina kneel on one knees. They kneel as the song goes, and get up. In the morning they dance the songs, and the afternoon they dance it all over the same way. It is dance at Christmas Day."

* * * * *

Nearly all the Matachines tunes are non-Indian in style. Three of the most characteristic are given herewith, of which the second and the third are particularly striking examples of this singular departure from the native manner. In addition to repetitions of the individual tunes, the music as a whole is repeated many times in the course of the dramatic action.

The reference numbers in the score pertain to the steps made by the two lines of Matachines, since their movements form the distinctive and continuous dance element of the ceremony. The principal steps, though simple, are rhythmically tricky. The most striking movement consists of a peculiar thrusting forward of the free foot while the knee is being lifted. This forward thrust occurs with every knee lift in which there is time to accomplish it; and sometimes it amounts to a little kick. Indication is made in the score, in the first and the second song, of a touch on the ground by one foot—while this is being done the feet are parallel, but the foot making the touch is several inches farther forward than the other foot. In certain measures of the second and of the third song occur turns, or revolutions. These are not accomplished by twisting on the foot, as in some other Indian turns, but by a simple stepping movement, as indicated in the score. The dancer follows the rhythm of his steps with his rattle and his trident. He moves the trident continuously across the body in front to right and left; the elbow leading the movement and thus causing the prongs of the trident to follow instead of precede the handle. The Matachines perform their steps for the greater part in place; the exception being an occasional walking in rhythm down the line, facing about, and walking back to place, with about eight steps in each direction. The tune to which this walking movement is made was not obtained; but an additional repetition of the third tune given herein would provide a satisfactory substitute in a reproduction of the dance.

The child dancer progresses with the same foot movements as those employed by the Matachines—*such* hard steps for a little maid to do so long in stiff United States boots!

† Miss Roberts's Indian informant gave her the following description of the costumes and the action of the Matachines as presented at Santa Clara Pueblo: "The dancers are all men except one little girl. The men wear a headdress and beads across their foreheads, with strings of them hanging down like a fringe to the chin. The beads are black and shiny. They wear a headdress shaped something like a priest's mitre with silver things on the front and a cross. They wear a silk handkerchief over their mouth. There is a lot of ribbons, all colors, twisted and looped on top of the headdress and hanging down their back. The mitre is made out of cowhide and covered with red cloth. They carry a three-forked stick in their left hand. In the right hand they carry a rattle made of tin, covered with a handkerchief. The three-forked stick is painted red or yellow, any kind they want, just so it look pretty. On their vests they have dimes, quarters, and any kinds of pins they have. They wear beaded moccasins and leggins with stripes beaded. They wear ordinary vests, or beaded ones, and arm bands and ordinary shirts of all colors. The man that goes in the centre and leads has a crown with a cap with straps in four places and a little cross standing upright in the centre made of silver. The cap is of cowskin and the crown of cowhide is fixed up with ribbons. Otherwise he is dressed like the other men. The men (perhaps five on each side) form two rows, sidewise to one another, and dance forward and back in their row. The leader stands in between them and goes the same way. The leader stands at the front of the rows. He is called Mananca. The little girl is called Malinche. The others are just called Matachinas dancers. The little girl, about six or seven years old, wears a wreath of flowers around her head (paper flowers) and a white veil hanging over her side head and back, but she is dressed in Indian, with white wrap boots and a white dress (woven) with embroidered border, and she has long feathers (of the parrot or macaw) at the back of her head which stick out forward. She follows the Mananca, dancing along. They also have some

funny people too, two men with masks, called Abuelo. The masks have a long nose. They are made of cowhide, painted any old way to look funny. They wear a long fringe on top of their heads, made of soft tanned cowhide, like a horse's mane. They wear ragged clothes, old overcoats, and boots like cowboys. They act funny to make the people laugh. They dance all around. They have a whip to drive the people back, like the war captains do at dances. Their whips are made of cowhide. They have a boy dressed up, with cowhide over his back, and cowhorns on his head, and another man beating the snare drum. There isn't any chorus. The boy with the cowhide is called the bull. The clowns are supposed to fight him. Another fellow shoots in the air with a gun when they kill the bull. When he falls down, the two clowns come over and butcher him. They fight the bull just as in Old Mexico. They try to make him mad and poke sticks at him and stick him, and keep on doing that. After a while the man shoots the gun in the air and he falls. Then they pretend to take the meat around after he is butchered and give it to the people. They don't drag him out like a dead bull at a bull fight. Then, after a while he gets up. They call him Toro. After they are through dancing in one place, along about four o'clock they go all around the pueblo, nearly, to each door, and then they are through. There are lots of Matachina songs played on the violin, but they are Mexican. There is only one Indian Matachina song sung at Santa Clara. The Mexicans also dance Matachina, but it is different. They wear citizen clothes. They borrow the headdress from the Indians."

MATACHINES

Song I

MATACHINES—Continued

Song II
(Given 3 Times)

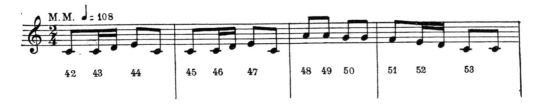

Song III
(Given 3 Times)

(Explanation of step reference-numbers in score.)

MATACHINES

Song I

(In place)

Preparation: The group dancers form in two lines, single file, facing forward.

1. Step on left foot, twisting to left until facing back, keeping right foot off ground.
2. Step on right foot, twisting to left, making quarter-turn.*
3. Twist on right foot until facing front.
4. Raise left foot and knee slightly; weight still on right foot.
5. Step on left foot and raise right knee high.
6. Touch right foot to ground a few inches forward; then raise it from ground, with knee high and a forward-thrust of the foot.*
7. Step on right foot, twisting to right until facing back, keeping left foot off ground.
8. Step on left foot, twisting to right, making quarter-turn.*
9. Twist on left foot until facing front.
10. Raise right foot and knee slightly; weight still on left foot.
11. Step on right foot and raise left foot, with knee high.
12. Touch left foot to ground a few inches forward; then raise it from ground, with knee high and a forward-thrust of the foot.*
13. Step on left foot.
14. Step on right foot.
15. Step on left foot.

16. Touch right foot to ground a few inches forward; keep weight on left foot.

17. Raise right foot and knee.

18. Touch right foot to ground a few inches forward.

19. Raise right foot and knee.

20. Touch right foot to ground a few inches forward.

21. Step on right foot.

22. Step on left foot.

23. Step on right foot.

24. Touch left foot to ground a few inches forward; keep weight on right foot.*

25. Step on left foot.

26. Step on right foot.

27. Step on left foot.

28. Touch right foot to ground a few inches forward; keep weight on left foot.*

Song II

(Given three times, in place)

First time:

29. Touch right foot to ground a few inches forward.

30. Touch right foot to ground a few inches forward.

31. Raise right knee, with a forward-thrust of the foot.

32. Step on right foot.

33. Step on left foot.

34. Step on right foot.

35. Touch left foot to ground a few inches forward.

---

* Teachers may find it expedient at times to simplify certain peculiar "off-beat" movements in Song I, in the following way:

At numbers 2, 6, 8, and 12, make the step *on*, instead of *after*, the first beat.
At numbers 24 and 28, make the step *on*, instead of *before*, the fourth beat.

36. Touch left foot to ground a few inches forward.

37. Raise left knee, with a forward-thrust of the foot.

38. Step on left foot.

39. Step on right foot.

40. Step on left foot.

41. In the following four measures, to double bar, duplicate movements 29–40 of preceding four measures.

Second time:

> The same as the first time, with the following exceptions:
>
> In the second measure, turn around to the left until facing back. Do not twist the feet to make this turn, but use for it the regular steps of the measure.
>
> Do the third measure still facing back.
>
> In the fourth measure, turn left until facing front again, using for the turn the regular steps of the measure.

Third time:

> The same as the second time, except that the turns are made to the right instead of to the left.

Song III
(Given three times, in place)

First time:

42. Step on right foot.

43. Step on left foot.

44. Step on right foot and raise left knee, with a forward-thrust of the left foot.

45. Step on left foot.

46. Step on right foot.

47. Step on left foot and raise right knee, with a forward-thrust of the right foot.

48. Step on right foot.

49. Step on left foot.

50. Step on right foot and raise left knee, with a forward-thrust of the left foot.

51. Step on left foot.

52. Step on right foot.

53. Step on left foot and raise right knee, with a forward-thrust of the right foot.

54. In the following four measures, duplicate movements 42–53 of preceding four measures.

55. Step on right foot.

Second time:

The same as the first time, with the following exceptions:

Begin on the left foot, and finish on the left foot.

Make a complete turn to the left in the course of the first three measures, using the regular steps.

Third time:

The same as the second time, with the following exceptions:

Begin on the right foot, and finish on the right foot.

The turn in the first three measures is to the right instead of to the left.

A YÉBICHAI DANCE FRAGMENT

The step and music given here are part of a dance known as the Yébichai. It is from the Night Chant, a great Navaho ceremonial. The Yébichai Dance has numerous sections. The following fragment is known to many Pueblo Indians as well as to the Navaho, though it is from a strictly Navaho ceremonial. It was observed first as danced by a group of Navaho, and later was learned in detail from Santo Domingo and San Ildefonso Indians. The dance as a whole was not obtained, the fragment given here comprising only a characteristic step and the accompanying music.

The dance is done partly in place, with a face-about at intervals; and partly in a movement of couples forming two lines and dancing down the middle, couple following couple—in figures and outlines not unlike a Virginia reel. The female rôles are usually impersonated by boys or men.

One form of step is used throughout the song. A quick slide, or "scrape," forward of a few inches, followed by a similar movement backward, is made on the ball of the left foot. With every slide forward of the left foot the right toe is lightly touched to the ground; and then the right foot is raised from the ground a little toward the back while the left foot is making its backward slide. When the dancers progress forward in the "reel" figure the advancement is achieved by making the forward slide cover a little more ground than the backward slide—a slow progress of only a few inches with each step. The general effect of the step is one of smoothness and ease. This is accomplished by letting the right toe, every time it touches the ground, carry some of the weight and thereby enable the left foot to make its scraping movement without hopping.

The step is difficult (for a white person) to learn. In the first attempt, the following method of practicing it will be found helpful: Hold on to a support of some kind (at each side if necessary). Raise the right foot from the ground in a slightly backward position. Keeping the right foot off the ground, slide the left foot a few inches forward, then backward. Continue this until balance is acquired and the movement becomes easy. Then add the touching of the right toe to the ground with every forward slide of the left foot (see fig. 11 a), and the slight lifting of the right foot from the ground a little toward the back with every backward slide of the left foot (see fig. 11 b). Once this is accomplished with ease, the step is in shape to be practiced without support.

In this dance there is no drum accompaniment. The dancers do the singing and use rattles. At times, usually at the end of a phrase, a tone is snapped off like a shrill yelp, as if suggested by the howling of the coyote. In the refrain of the song the singer bursts out into the strange cry of the Yébichai—"O ho ho ho! E he he he!"

Altogether, the Yébichai—with its group of performers engrossed in vehement song and emphatic step—is tremendously wild and vital.

A YÉBICHAI DANCE FRAGMENT

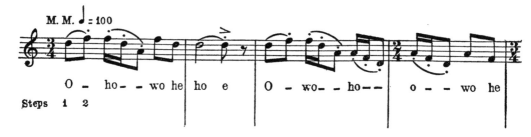

O - ho - - wo he ho e   O - wo - - ho - -   o - - wo he

Steps   1   2

ho e   He ya e lo   he ya he ya lo   ya - e lo   he ya he ya lo

·ya - e lo   he ya he ya lo He   o ho ho ho   e he he he

O ho ho ho   e he he he - -   O ho ho ho   e he he he - -

(Explanation of step reference-numbers in score.)

A YÉBICHAI DANCE FRAGMENT

The dancers form in two lines, in single file. When meeting as partners at the head of the lines they face about, and the couples dance down the centre. Preparation: Stand on ball of left foot. Raise right foot behind.

1. Slide forward a few inches on ball of left foot with a kind of scraping movement; at same time touch right toe to ground, and let it carry part of the weight.

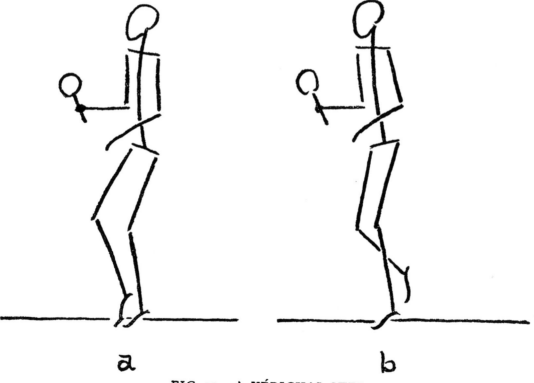

a   b

FIG. 11—A YÉBICHAI STEP

2. Slide back on ball of left foot with the same scraping movement as before; at same time raise right foot behind.

. A slow progress is achieved by making the forward movement cover slightly more ground than the backward one.

Continue movements 1 and 2 throughout, *without* alternation; and with the same time-value—that is, every forward slide has the value of an 8th-note, and every backward slide has the value of an 8th-note.

3. The dancers face about for repetition.

DOG DANCE

As an example of the confusion that often attends an initial effort in the study of Indian ceremonial, the writers' own experience may be cited. A friendly and artistic young Indian woman of San Ildefonso Pueblo sent word that on a certain date the tribe would give the Dog Dance. The ceremony, as is usual with Indian dances, was given out-of-doors. It was on a freezing day in January. The dance was done by two men whose bare legs and bodies were painted black; as were their faces also. In the right hand each carried a decorated rattle, and in the left a stick ornamented with a strip of gay cloth and dangling feathers. A great feather headdress extended from top to toe in the back. The dancers were accompanied by a splendidly attired choir of singers and drummers. (Sometimes, it was learned, each dancer has a long sash tied to his belt and held by an Indian woman, as if on a leash.)

At the close of the dance an Indian appeared from one of the little adobe houses of the Pueblo and threw a loaf of bread to the dancers, who got down on all fours, so to speak, and grubbed on the ground after the bread with their mouths. Finally one of them succeeded in catching the loaf securely between his teeth and carried it in this way to a singer in the choir, who relieved him of it. Another Indian came out of a house with another loaf, and the "scrap" was repeated. Then some bystanders—not Indians—threw small change; whereupon the dancers grovelled again on the ground, and, after rooting about vigorously, came up with coins between their teeth and their mouths choked with the dry soil. Not an edifying spectacle, this part, however realistic.

"What does the dance mean?" one of the drummers was asked.

"Peace," he replied.

"Why, a dog-fight over a loaf of bread doesn't seem a very peaceful ending," was the comment of the puzzled inquirers.

The drummer smiled his inscrutable Indian smile and said nothing.

"Why do the dogs carry the sticks with feathers?" was the next query.

"They are shields or banners," was the answer.

"Does the food belong in the ceremony?"

"Yes, food belongs," said the Indian.

"Do the coins belong?"

"No," he said, "Mexicans throw coins." (That was somewhat of a relief; for the unpleasant coin feature seemed hardly akin to the picturesque whimsey of occasional Indian comedy.)

"What is the right name of the dance?" the Indian was asked.

"It is called Dog Dance; but it is Peace Dance," was the calm response.

Peace! There *was* no peace—there was only a stubborn determination to track those two dogs to their lair. At first, hopefully following the peace clue, the inquirers were heartened in their search by coming across (in the official program of a Santa Fé fiesta) a graphic description that tallied admirably with the dance given at San Ildefonso Pueblo. The ceremonial described was a "Tanoan Peace Dance—part of an ancient Peace Drama, in which two dancers, representing the chiefs of opposing forces, stage a mimic combat, and description in movement of the battle that brought peace to the tribe. It goes back to the time when war issues were often settled among the people by single combat between opposing leaders. Sometimes the wife of each chief appears, holding a cord attached to the belt of each, showing how ties of home and family life moved men to valor in battle."

Back again to the San Ildefonso tribe for further persistent questioning:

"Where did the Dog Dance come from?" one of the Indians was asked.

"It did not come from any place," was the answer. "My father said it has been dance here for years and we still dance it yet. I have seen it dance the same way as it dance now since I was a small boy."

"Are the two men who do the dance supposed to represent dogs?"

"Yes, the two men represent as dogs while they are dancing—till it's over!"

"What does the Dog Dance mean?"

"It don't mean anything much. It's just call Dog Dance."

"Why is it called Dog Dance?"

"Because it was named it Dog Dance by the old people when they first dance it. They were painted all black and look like dogs."

"Does an Indian woman sometimes hold the dancer by a long sash tied to his belt? And what does it mean?"

"Yes, sometime the two dogs has a Indian belt tied to his belt and held by the women. They use the women same time so they can dance too. They carry the dogs around so they wouldn't run away."

"Why is the Dog Dance called also Peace Dance?"

"There is no dance here call Peace Dance. The Peace Dance is dance by the Taos Indians. It is almost the same as the Dog Dance."

Back of all these conflicting versions there is probably a very ancient symbolic ceremonial whose origin is lost in the obscurity of a remote past. Researches by eminent authorities show that the dog dance idea is widespread among tribes of the Plains Indians, and may have filtered through from them to the Pueblos of the Southwest, in one form or another. Dr. Clark Wissler, for example, describes (in his *Societies and Dance Associations of the Blackfeet Indians*) ceremonials, customs (including the food feature), and costumes of the Dog Societies of Plains Indians that would seem to establish definitely the kinship of the various "dogs" in Indian dances. And Pliny Earle Goddard (in his *Dancing Societies of the Sarsi Indians*) notes that in the dances of the Dog Society the wives of the members joined in, dancing behind their husbands; the wives of the leaders holding the ends of the long sashes as they danced.

Whatever its origin, and whether the dancers represent great chieftains dancing the dance of peace or (as is more probable) huge black dogs moving about with their lithe bodies in sinuous curves, the Dog Dance of San Ildefonso Pueblo is a remarkably effective impersonation. Not even the ensuing fight over coins mars its plastic beauty; for, happily, this feature is not introduced until the dance proper is over.

The principal movement in the dance consists in a nimble stepping forward or backward or in circles as each dancer advances toward or retreats from his opponent. The action is not difficult or peculiar in any way. It is just a continuous "soft," free stepping about—always graceful and light of foot; never jerky. Though through the greater part of the dance the two men are face to face (moving either toward each other as in fig. 12 a, or away from each other as in fig. 12 b), at intervals they turn away and move about in small individual circles. At certain times the dancers advance close to each other and pause a second, while each defiantly raises his shield (or banner?) aloft with emphasis (see fig. 12 c). The shield is usually held at the middle of the stick; but sometimes it is held by one end. The dance is repeated many times.

When each man is held on a leash by a woman, the latter follows the man with the same kind of step as that used by him. Each woman adorns herself for the dance according to her own fancy. She lets her hair hang loose. Besides holding the leash in one hand, she carries two feathers in each hand.

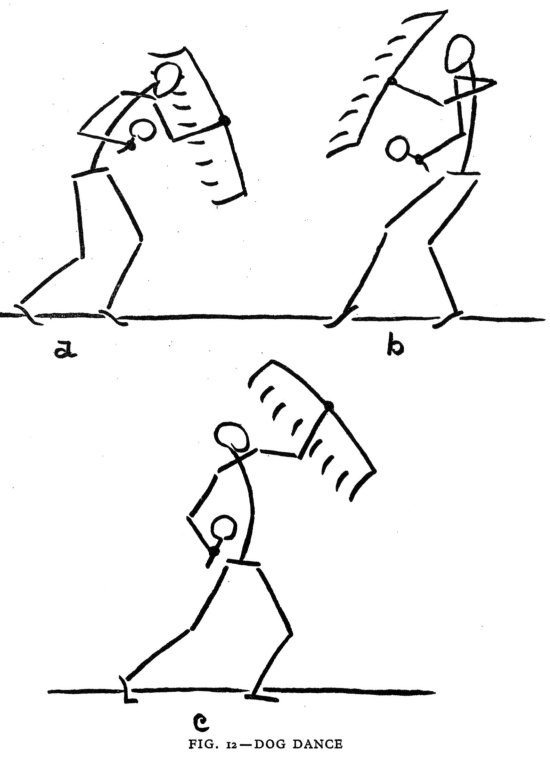

a

b

c

FIG. 12—DOG DANCE

>>

(Explanation of step reference-numbers in score.)

DOG DANCE

1. Step lightly on ball of right foot.
2. Step lightly on ball of left foot.

   Continue movements 1 and 2, with alternation, and with same time-value, a step to each quarter-note (while advancing, retreating, or circling), until movement number 3 is reached.

3. Pause and hold up shield, in a charging position; with the weight on the front foot.

4 and 5. Resume movements 1 and 2 (while advancing, retreating, or circling) and continue until movement number 6 is reached.

6. Pause and hold up shield, as in number 3.

>>

DOG DANCE

INDEX

INDEX

INDEX

INDEX

A CATALOG OF SELECTED
DOVER BOOKS
IN ALL FIELDS OF INTEREST

A CATALOG OF SELECTED DOVER
BOOKS IN ALL FIELDS OF INTEREST

CONCERNING THE SPIRITUAL IN ART, Wassily Kandinsky. Pioneering work by father of abstract art. Thoughts on color theory, nature of art. Analysis of earlier masters. 12 illustrations. 80pp. of text. 5⅜ x 8½.   23411-8

ANIMALS: 1,419 Copyright-Free Illustrations of Mammals, Birds, Fish, Insects, etc., Jim Harter (ed.). Clear wood engravings present, in extremely lifelike poses, over 1,000 species of animals. One of the most extensive pictorial sourcebooks of its kind. Captions. Index. 284pp. 9 x 12.   23766-4

CELTIC ART: The Methods of Construction, George Bain. Simple geometric techniques for making Celtic interlacements, spirals, Kells-type initials, animals, humans, etc. Over 500 illustrations. 160pp. 9 x 12. (Available in U.S. only.)   22923-8

AN ATLAS OF ANATOMY FOR ARTISTS, Fritz Schider. Most thorough reference work on art anatomy in the world. Hundreds of illustrations, including selections from works by Vesalius, Leonardo, Goya, Ingres, Michelangelo, others. 593 illustrations. 192pp. 7⅛ x 10¼.   20241-0

CELTIC HAND STROKE-BY-STROKE (Irish Half-Uncial from "The Book of Kells"): An Arthur Baker Calligraphy Manual, Arthur Baker. Complete guide to creating each letter of the alphabet in distinctive Celtic manner. Covers hand position, strokes, pens, inks, paper, more. Illustrated. 48pp. 8¼ x 11.   24336-2

EASY ORIGAMI, John Montroll. Charming collection of 32 projects (hat, cup, pelican, piano, swan, many more) specially designed for the novice origami hobbyist. Clearly illustrated easy-to-follow instructions insure that even beginning papercrafters will achieve successful results. 48pp. 8¼ x 11.   27298-2

THE COMPLETE BOOK OF BIRDHOUSE CONSTRUCTION FOR WOODWORKERS, Scott D. Campbell. Detailed instructions, illustrations, tables. Also data on bird habitat and instinct patterns. Bibliography. 3 tables. 63 illustrations in 15 figures. 48pp. 5¼ x 8½.   24407-5

BLOOMINGDALE'S ILLUSTRATED 1886 CATALOG: Fashions, Dry Goods and Housewares, Bloomingdale Brothers. Famed merchants' extremely rare catalog depicting about 1,700 products: clothing, housewares, firearms, dry goods, jewelry, more. Invaluable for dating, identifying vintage items. Also, copyright-free graphics for artists, designers. Co-published with Henry Ford Museum & Greenfield Village. 160pp. 8¼ x 11.   25780-0

HISTORIC COSTUME IN PICTURES, Braun & Schneider. Over 1,450 costumed figures in clearly detailed engravings—from dawn of civilization to end of 19th century. Captions. Many folk costumes. 256pp. 8⅜ x 11¾.   23150-X

THE STORY OF THE TITANIC AS TOLD BY ITS SURVIVORS, Jack Winocour (ed.). What it was really like. Panic, despair, shocking inefficiency, and a little heroism. More thrilling than any fictional account. 26 illustrations. 320pp. 5⅜ x 8½.
20610-6

FAIRY AND FOLK TALES OF THE IRISH PEASANTRY, William Butler Yeats (ed.). Treasury of 64 tales from the twilight world of Celtic myth and legend: "The Soul Cages," "The Kildare Pooka," "King O'Toole and his Goose," many more. Introduction and Notes by W. B. Yeats. 352pp. 5⅜ x 8½.
26941-8

BUDDHIST MAHAYANA TEXTS, E. B. Cowell and others (eds.). Superb, accurate translations of basic documents in Mahayana Buddhism, highly important in history of religions. The Buddha-karita of Asvaghosha, Larger Sukhavativyuha, more. 448pp. 5⅜ x 8½.
25552-2

ONE TWO THREE . . . INFINITY: Facts and Speculations of Science, George Gamow. Great physicist's fascinating, readable overview of contemporary science: number theory, relativity, fourth dimension, entropy, genes, atomic structure, much more. 128 illustrations. Index. 352pp. 5⅜ x 8½.
25664-2

EXPERIMENTATION AND MEASUREMENT, W. J. Youden. Introductory manual explains laws of measurement in simple terms and offers tips for achieving accuracy and minimizing errors. Mathematics of measurement, use of instruments, experimenting with machines. 1994 edition. Foreword. Preface. Introduction. Epilogue. Selected Readings. Glossary. Index. Tables and figures. 128pp. 5⅜ x 8½. 40451-X

DALÍ ON MODERN ART: The Cuckolds of Antiquated Modern Art, Salvador Dalí. Influential painter skewers modern art and its practitioners. Outrageous evaluations of Picasso, Cézanne, Turner, more. 15 renderings of paintings discussed. 44 calligraphic decorations by Dalí. 96pp. 5⅜ x 8½. (Available in U.S. only.)
29220-7

ANTIQUE PLAYING CARDS: A Pictorial History, Henry René D'Allemagne. Over 900 elaborate, decorative images from rare playing cards (14th–20th centuries): Bacchus, death, dancing dogs, hunting scenes, royal coats of arms, players cheating, much more. 96pp. 9¼ x 12¼.
29265-7

MAKING FURNITURE MASTERPIECES: 30 Projects with Measured Drawings, Franklin H. Gottshall. Step-by-step instructions, illustrations for constructing handsome, useful pieces, among them a Sheraton desk, Chippendale chair, Spanish desk, Queen Anne table and a William and Mary dressing mirror. 224pp. 8⅛ x 11¼.
29338-6

THE FOSSIL BOOK: A Record of Prehistoric Life, Patricia V. Rich et al. Profusely illustrated definitive guide covers everything from single-celled organisms and dinosaurs to birds and mammals and the interplay between climate and man. Over 1,500 illustrations. 760pp. 7½ x 10⅛.
29371-8

Paperbound unless otherwise indicated. Available at your book dealer, online at **www.doverpublications.com**, or by writing to Dept. GI, Dover Publications, Inc., 31 East 2nd Street, Mineola, NY 11501. For current price information or for free catalogues (please indicate field of interest), write to Dover Publications or log on to **www.doverpublications.com** and see every Dover book in print. Dover publishes more than 500 books each year on science, elementary and advanced mathematics, biology, music, art, literary history, social sciences, and other areas.